Praise for *Chase the Bears*

"Ric Keller hits just the right note in *Chase the Bears* ᴺ᷾᷾᷾ nly is it engaging, inspiring, and funny, but it ᵗ ᵎ d plan for achieving their dreams. 1

— **Jack Canfield,** coau ᵎᵎᵎ lling *Chicken Soup for* ᵎ ʳⁱnciples

"*Chase the Bears* is a gem of a book that everyone will enjoy and find benefit in. With humility and humor, Ric Keller guides us to pursue our dreams and find happiness not through blind ambition, but rather through character and relationships."

— **Arthur C. Brooks,** professor, Harvard Kennedy School and Harvard Business School, and #1 *New York Times* bestselling author

"*Chase the Bears* inspires you to use your gifts and take action. You are where you are today based on the choices you made before today. If you want something different, simply start making different choices. The greatest risk of all is to take no action. The stories are heartfelt and inspiring, and also humorous!"

— **Sharon Lechter,** coauthor of the #1 *New York Times* bestselling *Rich Dad Poor Dad, Think and Grow Rich for Women,* and 17 other books

"If you want to network the right way–and achieve your highest potential–read *Chase the Bears*. Ric Keller's book is insightful, useful, and—best of all—incredibly witty and a pleasure to read."

— **Dorie Clark,** *Wall Street Journal* bestselling author of *The Long Game* and executive education faculty, Duke University Fuqua School of Business

"Ric has a great sense of humor. *Chase the Bears* shows why leading with boldness, civility, and a little humor will make you a leader worth following. It's a fun read."

—**Jeb Bush,** former Governor of Florida

"The only things that will change you from where you are today to where you'll be five years from now are the books you read, the people you meet, and the dreams you dream. Ric Keller's new book, *Chase the Bears,* will definitely change your life for the positive in the next five years!"

—**Lou Holtz,** national championship head football coach
at the University of Notre Dame

"*Chase the Bears* inspires you to trust your intuition. It can change your life . . . and maybe the world."

—**Michael Smerconish,** SiriusXM and CNN host

"Every new day gives you the opportunity to change direction and head on a path to achieve your dreams. *Chase the Bears* will show you the tips, techniques, and practical actions to take your thoughts and aspirations and convert them into reality. Ric Keller's book is wise, witty, and truly inspirational."

—**Brittany Wagner,** nationally respected athletic academic counselor, motivational speaker, star of the hit Netflix documentary series, *Last Chance U,* and author of *Next Chance You*

"I first met Ric Keller when we were both new members of Congress and always valued his intelligence and his ability to see the big picture. Ric is a fine leader who understands the importance of mentoring, which is one of the values we share. I have devoted the last thirty years of my life working at mentoring. I think that you will enjoy reading *Chase the Bears* as leadership and mentoring are huge factors with our young people today."

—**Tom Osborne,** three-time national championship head football coach at the University of Nebraska

"Ric Keller has written a tremendous new book, *Chase the Bears.* The term, chase the bears, is often a metaphor for chasing your dreams. In my own life, I have learned that chasing dreams takes hard work and involves risks. But in the end, the biggest risk of all is to simply take no risks. I urge you to read Ric Keller's new book and let his experiences help you create the life you are dreaming of."

—**Don Green,** executive director, The Napoleon Hill Foundation

Chase the Bears

LITTLE THINGS TO ACHIEVE
BIG DREAMS

Ric Keller

Health Communications, Inc.
Boca Raton, Florida

www.hcibooks.com

Orlando Sentinel photograph reprinted with permission. ©Orlando Sentinel/TCA

"An Ode to the Big Tree" used with permission. ©Paul A. Peterzell

Cover photograph used with permission. ©Steve Vaughn Photography

Library of Congress Cataloging-in-Publication Data
is available through the Library of Congress

© 2022 Ric Keller

ISBN-13: 978-07573-2448-2 (Paperback)
ISBN-10: 07573-2448-7 (Paperback)
ISBN-13: 978-07573-2449-9 (ePub)
ISBN-10: 07573-2449-5 (ePub)

Publisher: Health Communications, Inc.
      301 Crawford Blvd., Suite 200
      Boca Raton, FL 33432-1653

Author photo ©Jeff Hawkins
Cover, interior design and formatting by Larissa Hise Henoch

To Lori, for inspiring me and for
secretly letting me win in Scrabble.
(You think I didn't know?)
To Grandma Lora, for making me
feel loved and for guiding me from Above.
To Linda, for being twice the stepmom
you didn't have to be.

Contents

INTRODUCTION:
Chase the Bears

One sunny Florida morning, my wife, Lori, and I were sitting at our kitchen table, sipping coffee and reading the newspaper. All of a sudden, a big mama bear and three cute little cubs scampered across our front yard just outside the kitchen window. It had never happened before; we lived in a condominium complex miles from any wooded areas. Without saying a word, we looked at each other, jumped up, and quickly ran outside to chase the bears.

It might not have been our smartest idea. Florida black bears can run up to 35 mph. In comparison, Olympic sprinters run only 28 mph. Black bears typically mind their own business and won't charge after you—unless you're foolish enough to chase them. And, of course, we were.

But it was an "educated risk." If the mama bear decided to turn around and charge after us, I knew the front door to our home was nearby. Plus, I was pretty sure I could outrun Lori.

Interestingly, we never saw the bears again; they had disappeared.

Afterward, we laughed. What did this say about us as a couple? Don't most couples have at least one person who is supposed to be rational? Shouldn't one of us have been the cautious one?

We also realized that "chasing the bears" is a metaphor in life for chasing your dreams. Most people are content to stay inside, play it safe, and look out their windows as life passes them by. Eventually, the clock runs out. On the other hand, a few people take a risk and chase their dreams. They "chase the bears."

This book is written for people who want to pursue their dreams and be happy. Spoiler alert: a huge part of that equation is deciding what YOU really want (not what your parents, spouse, friends, or coworkers want), and then—once you are aligned with your purpose—use your gifts, trust your instincts, and take risks to achieve one baby-step goal at a time.

Why did I write this book?

This book is very personal for me. I didn't meet my father until I was fourteen years old. At our first meeting, he handed me a newly purchased paperback copy of his favorite book, titled *Think and Grow Rich*, by Napoleon Hill. Unbeknownst to him, I would read it six times before graduating from high school.

It would take me another three years until I was ready to call him "Dad" and to finally put the book's secret formula to a practical test. I was going off to college, and as an experiment, I set a goal to graduate first in my class with a 4.0 GPA, despite being an average student in high school. It happened. The second experiment was setting a goal to get elected to Congress. That happened, too.

Of course, like anyone else, there were also plenty of setbacks. But I learned that if you can laugh at yourself and at life, you will be *unstoppable*.

I've been to hell and back—and took notes. What I know for sure is that there are little things you can do to achieve big dreams. I hope this book can change your life just like that gift book from Dad changed mine.

If you aspire to leadership, I will share lessons I learned from my dealings with CEOs, generals, Supreme Court justices, government leaders, and a legendary college football coach about the common denominators of great leaders, including boldness, authenticity, and civility.

I hope you use your gifts, trust your instincts, and take educated risks to achieve your dreams. I know that even if someone is poor, raised by a single mom, and doesn't have any rich friends or political connections, they, too, can go to college, become a lawyer, get elected to Congress, or achieve whatever they personally desire.

This book is not about politics. It is about the success principles that are equally applicable to people who pursue careers in business, sports, or entertainment. I'll tell you how to apply secret techniques to convert your thoughts and dreams into reality. This book tells you where to turn, what to do, and how to do it.

The book is divided into two sections: Connecting Your Gifts to Your Goals, and Connecting with People. In Part One, we'll start with the importance of discovering your gifts, trusting your intuition, and setting specific goals that are aligned with your purpose. We'll also discuss taking actions to move toward your dreams by taking educated risks and making persistent efforts to achieve each baby-step goal. Plus, we'll talk about focusing on one major goal at a time, and why it's important to pivot or make "half-time adjustments" to your plans to achieve your dream.

Part Two is about connecting with people and cultivating authentic long-term relationships. We'll discuss how to network with people the right way and the differences between mentors and sponsors. We'll also talk about how leading with boldness, civility, humility, and a little humor will make you a leader worth following.

Chase the Bears is not meant to be a book you simply skim through and walk away from unchanged. To get the most out of the book, read each chapter to get a bird's eye view of it. As you read, use a highlighter or pen to underscore every sentence that impresses you favorably. Then go back and reread each chapter thoroughly, again underscoring each sentence that speaks to you. I encourage you to stop and reflect on those specific sentences and pay particular attention to the three-step formula outlined in Chapter 2.

You were given a dream that was placed in your imagination by God (or the Universe, Infinite Intelligence, Divine Intelligence, or whatever term you use for the all-powerful creative life force). And, at birth, you were given the very gift you need to achieve your dream.

Believe me, I am an ordinary, not extraordinary, person. If I can do it, then you can, too.

The "Shadow of the Bear" photo on the book cover is from Whiteside Mountain near Cashiers, North Carolina, with the highest rock cliffs east of the Rockies.[1] It's a naturally occurring phenomenon that doesn't happen anywhere else in the world.

The bear's shadow makes its appearance from mid-October through early November for thirty minutes (on sunny days) at about 5:30 PM. It then goes into "hibernation" until it reappears briefly in mid-February to early March.[2] A photographer friend of mine, Steve Vaughn, traveled to western North Carolina to try to catch a glimpse of the "bear" and, as luck would have it, snapped this photograph at the perfect moment.

The "shadow of the bear" is a relevant metaphor because we are only given a limited amount of time to pursue our dreams. If we hesitate before moving or neglect to act soon enough, we can miss our opportunity; the clock runs out. We need to have the courage to take advantage of opportunities when they arise, as those opportunities may not last.

Imagine yourself standing on top of that tall cliff (above the bear's shadow), and inside your backpack is a parachute. That parachute is your unique gift (your skill or talent).

You've got a decision to make. If you jump, you will feel alive, use your gift, and soar in the direction of your dreams. On the other hand, you can choose to play it safe, stay on top of the cliff, and avoid any risk of getting hurt. However, if you take the safe route, the one guarantee you have is that your parachute will never open, and you'll die with it on your back.

What should you do? Steve Harvey, the Emmy Award-winning host of TV's *Family Feud* game show, described the above analogy in his book *Jump*.[3] He continues, "Every successful person has jumped. You have to take that gift that is packed away in your backpack, jump off the cliff, and pull the cord."[4] Later in this book, you'll read a detailed account of Steve Harvey's inspirational story and learn how Dolly Parton, Jim Carrey, and many other well-known high achievers used the same secret success principles and techniques to achieve their dreams.

It's not too late. You can still be what you wish to be. Colonel Sanders didn't open his first Kentucky Fried Chicken franchise until he was sixty-two years old. Most importantly, when you get the choice in life to "play it safe" or chase the bears—*I hope you chase the freaking bears!* Let's go!

Ric Keller
Winter Park, Florida

part ONE

CONNECTING YOUR GIFTS TO YOUR GOALS

CHAPTER 1
Use Your Gifts

*"Your gift is that thing you do the absolute best
with the least amount of effort."*

—Steve Harvey

What do you really want? Not what your parents, spouse, friends, or coworkers want. What do you really want? Asking yourself this question is the first step toward self-fulfillment.

Your mission in life, if you choose to accept it, is to use your gift to make other peoples' lives better. Hence, your gift (i.e., talent) provides the ultimate clue as to what it is you really want. Your gift is that thing you do well, you love doing it, and it comes easy for you without much effort. When you do that thing, it puts you in a better mood, time flies, and you serve others.

When someone says, "You can do anything you want in life," it's partially BS. The reality is you can achieve anything you want in life, but only if you stay in your lane and use your gift. "Do that which is assigned you, and you cannot hope too much or dare too much," said Ralph Waldo Emerson. If Albert Einstein had tried to be a professional bull rider instead of a Nobel Prize-winning physicist, he would have landed $E = MC$ square on his butt in less than eight seconds!

Dolly Parton: "Dumb Blonde" Takes It to the Bank

Dolly Parton is a good example of someone who knew what she wanted and used her gifts to get it. On the night she graduated from high school, students were asked what they planned to do with their lives. Parton said, "I'm going to Nashville to be a star." The other students laughed. It didn't shake her; the day after graduation she left for Nashville. She went on to record twenty-five number-one songs on the country charts.[5]

Early in her career, Parton gave up her job on the popular *Porter Wagoner* TV show to pursue a solo career. As a farewell tribute to Wagoner, she wrote the song "I Will Always Love You." After her song hit number one on the country chart, Elvis Presley's manager, Col. Tom Parker, informed her that Elvis loved the song so much he wanted to record it, too. Parton was thrilled because Elvis was one of the biggest stars in the world at the time, as well as a hero of hers.

Unfortunately, on the day before Elvis was set to record it, the manager told Parton that she would have to sign over half of her songwriting royalties to Elvis. "Something in my heart said don't do that," said Parton, who mustered up the courage to turn down The King.[6]

Her friends thought she was crazy, but that bold decision would one day make her quite wealthy. Many years later, Kevin Costner, the Hollywood actor and director, asked and received Parton's permission to allow Whitney Houston to record "I Will Always Love You" for the movie *The Bodyguard* (with Dolly retaining 100 percent of the royalties).

Houston's cover became the number-one bestselling single by a female artist of all time. Parton joked, "When I recorded it, I put money in the bank. When Whitney recorded it, I bought the bank."[7]

After her success on the country charts, Parton decided she wanted to cross over into pop music, television, and movies. She accepted an acting role in the movie *9 to 5* on the condition that they allow her to write and sing the movie's theme song. The "9 to 5" song reached number one on the pop charts, and the movie was a smash hit at the box office.

Next, she wanted to expand her entertainment empire and open an amusement park called Dollywood in the Great Smoky Mountains. Some thought she had lost her mind.[8] Dollywood is now more popular than Disneyland (according to Tripadvisor), and she has a reported net worth of over $600 million to go along with the ten Grammy Awards on her mantel.[9]

Parton succeeded because she knew what she wanted in life and used her musical gifts—along with her larger-than-life personality, appearance, and quick wit—to make her dreams come true. When people suggested she was a dumb blonde, she laughed it off and said, "I know I'm not dumb, and I know I'm not blonde."

Jim Carrey: Dumb and Dumber or Smart and Smarter?

Jim Carrey is another funny entertainer who "chased the bears." Carrey's father could have been a great comedian but instead took a "safe" job as an accountant. When Carrey was twelve years old, his father got let go from that safe job, and the family struggled to survive. It taught Carrey a valuable lesson: "You can fail at what you don't want, so you might as well take a chance on doing what you love."[10]

With this lesson in mind, the young Canadian actor and comedian took a chance and moved to Hollywood to pursue his dream. Before he became famous, Carrey wrote himself a check for $10 million for "acting services rendered" and dated it Thanksgiving 1995. He kept the check in his wallet and imagined movie directors wanting to work with him. Just before Thanksgiving 1995, he was offered the lead role in *Dumb and Dumber* for *$10 million*. When his father passed away, Carrey slipped the check into his casket as a final tribute to the man who inspired his success.[11]

Don't Live Someone Else's Dream

Dolly Parton and Jim Carrey both embraced their gifts and chased their dreams, not someone else's. Life is short. Don't waste your life living someone else's dream. For example, don't go to medical school because your parents want you to. Instead, do what *you* really want.

I speak from firsthand experience as someone who screwed it up. Hoping to make my parents proud of me, I decided in high school I wanted to become a doctor.

I attended East Tennessee State University (ETSU) on a public speaking scholarship, and I took pre-med courses and also majored in speech communications. I loved the public speaking courses but hated the science classes. Nevertheless, I pulled lots of coffee-fueled, all-night study sessions to keep my grades up in all the tough classes, such as organic chemistry and physics.

Fast forward to graduation day. There was good news and bad news for my parents. The good news was I did graduate number one in my class with a 4.0 GPA. The bad news was that I had volunteered at a hospital during my senior year and found out I hated everything about it—the sight of blood, the smell of disinfectant in the hallways, and the sounds of the cranky patients. I felt so dumb. How could I just be figuring this out after four years?

I did know some things. In terms of my gifts, I knew I loved public speaking, that I could take complicated things and communicate them in a way that is easy to understand, and that I loved using humor to relax people and build rapport. I did those things well with very little energy.

I also knew I wanted to use my gifts to help people. For example, I was passionate about helping students from low-income families go to college, mainly because I was raised by a single mom and didn't have enough money to go to college. It was only because of federal financial aid (Pell Grants) and the generosity of my mom's eighty-one-year-old boss that I was able to cobble together enough money to go to college. It gave me a good feeling that, as a member of Congress, I could possibly use my gifts and help kids go to college. I also knew that, for better or worse, most congressional lawmakers (including Abe Lincoln) were lawyers.

My Decision Point

The bottom line was my logic told me I should go to medical school, but my *intuition* told me to go into law and politics. It was a fork in the road. The *mother* of all forks in the road. A mother-forking dilemma.

Of course, I wasn't the first person to question one's original job choice. According to *Forbes* magazine, the number-one job that five-year-old kids want is not to be a doctor or lawyer; it's Spider-Man.[12]

Still, I faced a tough decision. I needed time to think it over. I took a year off between college and graduate school, moved to New York, and got a job as a counselor at a welfare-to-work job training program. After a year, I was still undecided about my future. The indecision was killing me.

And then an idea popped into my head. I drove alone to the Pocono Mountains in eastern Pennsylvania, pitched a tent in the middle of the woods, climbed inside, and waited for that "still, small voice" to guide me to the proper answer. Instead of hearing a voice *inside* my head, I heard the grunt of a bear *outside* my tent. It scared the hell out of me. I sprinted to my nearby car so fast I probably could have made the Olympic track team!

I drove into town, found a local pub, and took a seat at the bar. The bartender handed me an ice-cold beer in a frosted mug. I took a big gulp of beer, followed by a few deep breaths. There was business at hand. I promised myself that I'd make a final decision that weekend. So, once again, I began to contemplate whether I should become a doctor or a lawyer/politician.

I asked for a sign. And I got one. I noticed a poster on the wall. It said a politician was hosting a barbecue the next day with free food. That was it. That was the moment I decided to go into politics.

Holy crap! If that barroom poster had said "The circus is coming to town," I might be a *lion tamer* right now! Instead of Siegfried and Roy, it could have been Siegfried and Ric!

My gut feeling told me to drive to the Poconos. A bear's grunt steered me toward the pub. And a poster provided the sign I needed. Granted, it wasn't the most *logical* decision-making process. But at least I had a decision. And it was *my* decision to use *my* gifts to *help others*.

I never looked back.

The Underdog

After deciding on law and politics, I got accepted into Vanderbilt Law School. After graduating, I practiced law for a few years in Orlando and made partner at my firm.

When I was thirty-four years old, I filed my papers to run for the U.S. Congress. There were a few problems. First, I didn't have any rich friends or political connections. Second, I had never run for office before and was unknown. And third, I was such an underdog that I literally could not pay people to work for me because they said I had "no chance."

Six months into the campaign, it was a disaster. The frontrunner was beating me in the polls by a jaw-dropping 27 percentage points. She had raised $400,000 compared to my $100,000. And the chairman of my own party asked me to drop out. I'm not saying I was dead, but that kid from the movie *The Sixth Sense* was able to see me.

My intuition told me to stay in the race, so I did. I trust my instincts no matter how unconventional or unpopular they seem. (You should, too.) I set a new fundraising goal of $400,000. I had no clue *how* I'd do it. But I wrote it down on my goal card (to be discussed in Chapter 2) and read it every night and every morning.

American Idol for Politicians

A few weeks later, I got a phone call. I was invited to Washington to give a five-minute speech. It was like *American Idol* for politicians. A newly formed group of CEOs and business leaders were considering putting some big money into a handful of congressional races. They had looked at hundreds of races across the country and narrowed the list down to sixteen finalists. I made the cut.

I flew to Washington the morning of the event. Before it started, I chatted backstage with my competitors, who included future Vice President Mike Pence and future Senator/Ambassador Jeff Flake. I then stood in the back of the room and waited my turn. The room was full of tension.

I was the *last* one to speak, and my *first* words were, "I've been waiting for a couple of hours. I feel like Elizabeth Taylor's seventh husband on his wedding night. Technically, I know what I'm *supposed* to do, but at this point, I don't know how to make it interesting." The room exploded with laughter. I spoke from the heart without any notes.

After the short talk was over, I pulled the name tag off my jacket and threw it into a trash can. My PAC fundraiser, Tom Hammond, ran over and snatched the name tag out of the trash and handed it back to me. He said, "Keep this, Ric. That speech just changed your life."

And he was right. That little icebreaker changed my whole life. The group ranked me number one in the country. They spent $400,000 to support me—the *exact* amount of my goal. And a few months later, against all odds, I won a seat in the United States Congress by a narrow margin of 51 percent to 49 percent.

The date was November 7, 2000. As a young Vanderbilt law student, I had written a note to my dad and stepmom on November 7, 1990, which said, "I plan on busting my ass to get elected to Congress." Ten years later, to the exact date, I was elected.

The Stage

It was now time to give my first election-night victory speech. I made it up onto the stage. For ten years, I had visualized myself up on this stage. In my imagination, people were cheering, signs were waving, flashbulbs were going off, and the TV cameras were rolling. Now, it was real life. And it was surreal. It was *exactly* how I imagined it would be.

Celebrating my underdog victory from the stage on election night with my supporters.

I didn't have a written speech prepared and didn't need one. After thanking everyone, I told the audience a little-known secret about an emotional turning point in my childhood. I was seventeen years old and didn't have enough money to go to college. My mom, a single parent, had worked as a secretary for Mr. R.T. Overstreet. He was eighty-one years old and president of the Overstreet Investment Company.

Over the years, Mr. Overstreet had often asked my mom to type up checks for various charitable contributions. Seeing this, Mom suggested that I meet with Mr. Overstreet and ask if his company would consider making a charitable contribution to help me pay for my college.

I was nervous. I walked into his large office, and he offered me a seat. I cut to the chase. I told Mr. Overstreet—with all the passion

I could muster—that I wanted a college education so badly, and I promised him that I would graduate number one in my class, with a perfect 4.0 GPA, if his company would only take a chance on me and help with college.

He told me that he would have to run my request by the board of directors. He asked me to come back next Tuesday. I couldn't sleep the night before the big day. I went to his office and awaited the decision. Mr. Overstreet informed me that his corporation would *not* be able to pay my college tuition. He said if the corporation paid for my education, they would have to do it for all the employees.

I thanked Mr. Overstreet for at least trying. And then, uncontrollably, tears started to run down my face. It hit me at that moment that my dream of getting a college education would never come true.

Mr. Overstreet then leaned toward me and said, "Son, you can wipe the tears away. I said the company couldn't pay for your college; I didn't say that I couldn't." With that, Mr. Overstreet cut a check and sent me to college. Four years later, I stood onstage and graduated top in my class. Mr. Overstreet lived just long enough to see me graduate from Vanderbilt Law School.

Graduation day at Vanderbilt
Law School in 1992.

As I spoke from the stage on election night, I imagined Mr. Overstreet looking down from heaven. I hoped he would be proud of me. I know I was proud of him. I couldn't possibly know it that night, but I would go on to become chairman of the House Higher Education Subcommittee and achieve my goal of increasing Pell Grants (college aid) by 62 percent—which helped more than five million students from low-income families go to college. Mr. Overstreet's single act of kindness had positively impacted five million lives.

Dreamers Make Things Happen

Napoleon Hill wrote, "Let no one influence you to scorn the dreamer." I'm writing this chapter from Orlando, the home of Walt Disney World, the dream of an extraordinary dreamer. At age twenty-two, Walt Disney was fired from his newspaper job as a cartoonist for "not being creative enough." His Mickey Mouse theme-park concept was rejected more than 300 times by bankers. Orlando is the tourism capital of the world simply because one visionary leader didn't let the critics shake his confidence. (It almost makes me cut him some slack for that "It's a Small World" song that gets stuck in my head. Almost.)

Martin Luther King Jr., whose "I Have a Dream" speech made history, once got a C in public speaking in seminary school.

Michael Jordan was cut from his high school basketball team.

The Beatles were rejected by Decca Records for not being good enough to make it in the record business.

Oprah Winfrey was once demoted from her job as a news anchor because she "wasn't fit for television."

Everybody knows the names of these great dreamers. Nobody remembers the names of the people who told Walt Disney, Dr. King, Michael Jordan, Oprah Winfrey, and the Fab Four they weren't good enough.

Forget the critics, but remember the adage: "Don't take criticism from someone you wouldn't take advice from." If the thing you wish to do is right, and it is aligned with your gifts, then go ahead and do it!

Take the Einstein Quiz

The pending question of this chapter is: What do you really want? Albert Einstein, best known for the world's most famous equation, $E=mc^2$, gave us all a valuable hint as to how we might solve problems. He said, "If I had an hour to solve a problem and my life depended on the solution, I would spend the first fifty-five minutes determining the proper question to ask. For once I know the proper question, I could solve the problem in less than five minutes."

Well, the quality of your life *does* depend on you solving this problem. To determine what it is you really want, the proper question to ask is: *What is my gift?* Your mission in life is to use your gift to make other people's lives better.

You can relax. You are just the *conduit*. Your future is in the hands of powers that are greater than yours (i.e., God, the Universe, Infinite Intelligence, or Divine Force). You are meant to use your gifts in service to others. When you do, life flows downstream, and you feel alive. When you don't, life blocks you at every turn and you feel depressed.

Quite simply, you were given a mission in life, and you were given a talent to fulfill that mission. If you do what you love, the Universe will conspire to help you. "A man's gift maketh room for him, and bringeth him before great men." PROVERBS 18:16 KJV.

Let's put it all together and conclude this chapter by taking the Einstein quiz. Like Einstein, you, too, can figure out the answer to what your gift is in *less than five minutes* by asking yourself these ten questions:

1. What do you do the absolute best with the least amount of effort?
2. What do you love doing?

3. What makes you feel alive?

4. What makes you lose track of time because time flies by?

5. What puts you in a better mood after you start doing it?

6. What is the gift that other people associate you with?

7. What job would you do for free?

8. What job would be the closest thing to not working?

9. What job would you do if you knew you would not fail?

10. What gift or talent do you have that helps others?

Do you have the same answer to nearly every question? If so, it seems that you and good ol' Einstein have cracked the code. Congratulations! You know your gift! Nothing is more important to your happiness than being aligned with your purpose.

That brings us to the key question: how do you unleash the power of goal-setting to make your dreams come true?

TAKEAWAY

"Your gift is that thing you do the absolute best with the least amount of effort," Steve Harvey said. Use your gift every day. Don't waste your gift or time living someone else's dream.

CHAPTER 2
Set Goals

"Whatever the mind of man can conceive
and believe, it can achieve."
—Napoleon Hill

How did Jim Carrey become a movie star? How did Steve Harvey become a television personality? How did I go from humble beginnings to Congress? We all used the most powerful goal-setting formula in the world. And you can harness this same power, too.

Three Steps to Convert Your Thoughts into Reality

This section is the single most important part of this book. The most powerful tools to convert your thoughts into reality are affirmations and visualizations. Three specific steps make up the secret formula of how to achieve your goals.

First, write down a specific goal on a card along with a *definite date* by when you expect to achieve it. It is key that you select a goal that is within the area of your gifts.

Second, read the goal card every morning when you rise and every night just before sleep. Your subconscious mind is most receptive to suggestions during these periods.

Third, *visualize* yourself already in possession of the goal as you read it. Act and feel *as if* you already have it. (If you have trouble visualizing it, use a photograph—this is the idea behind vision boards.)

It's critical that you are specific. Vague goals bring vague results. Dreams are more specific and effective than wishes. For example, a wish is: "It would be cool to be a famous entertainer." A dream is: "I will be an actress on Broadway before I'm thirty."

Similarly, instead of saying, "I want to lose weight in the future," it's better to say, "I will weigh 185 pounds by February 1, 2023."

In my experience, it will take you three to four weeks after you begin reading your goal card to get the mental train rolling, but after that, the engine will drive you the rest of the way. Keep reading it. Keep visualizing it. Don't take your foot off the pedal until you realize your goal.

I am confident in your ability to use these three steps to achieve your goals because I have road tested them in my own life and converted my thoughts into reality. I put the secret formula to a practical test with two goal experiments: graduating first in my class with a 4.0 GPA, and getting elected to Congress. Both happened.

I first learned about these techniques by reading Napoleon Hill's classic book, *Think and Grow Rich*. Hill's book, written in 1937 during the Great Depression, gave people much-needed hope that they truly could think and grow rich; it may well be the most influential self-help book of all time. Beyond obtaining wealth, these three steps are essential to the achievement of *any* specific goal, including getting good grades, winning a seat in Congress, losing weight, becoming a famous performer, winning a gold medal, selling insurance, launching or expanding a business, becoming a champion athlete, writing a bestseller, or delivering inspirational speeches.

The following are among those who have read *Think and Grow Rich* and attribute their success to having applied these same principles: singers Billy Ray Cyrus, Lana Del Rey, Dolly Parton, and Kendrick Lamar; television personalities Steve Harvey, Oprah Winfrey, and Daymond John; actors Arnold Schwarzenegger, Jim Carrey, and Matthew McConaughey; authors/speakers Tony Robbins, Jack Canfield, Don Green, and Bob Proctor; and boxing champs Ken Norton and Anthony Joshua.[13]

Why Affirmations and Visualizations Work

Here's why affirmations and visualizations work: achievements require confidence. Confidence requires belief. Repeating affirmations and visualizations will help you to *believe* it. In other words, by saying specific affirmations to yourself over and over, you will eventually come to believe them. It is a well-known fact that you come to believe whatever you repeat to yourself, regardless of whether it is true or false.

The technique is called *autosuggestion*. Autosuggestion allows you to reach and influence your subconscious mind. Your subconscious mind is your link to that abundant source of power that is greater than yourself (i.e., God, the Universe, Infinite Intelligence, or Divine Force). Whatever you give to your subconscious mind, it will work night and day to achieve it.

Similarly, visualization is a powerful tool in creating belief because your brain cannot distinguish between what is real or illusory. In other words, imaginary "mind movies" convince or "trick" your subconscious mind into believing that your desired result is real, tangible, possible, and even already in existence.

When you utilize affirmations and visualizations, you will begin meeting people who can help you fulfill your mission. Work with them. Ideas and plans will pop into your mind as flashes of inspiration. Write them down. Opportunities will arise. Take them. Doors will open. Walk through them; don't hesitate.

Baby Steps: Breaking Down the Dream

Although I always have a long-term goal in mind, I find that breaking my goal card down into small steps, typically three to six months out, works best.

For example, my first big goal was to graduate number one in my class in college with a 4.0 GPA. However, since I was just a mediocre student when I set that goal, the long-term overall goal was way too much for my brain to handle on a daily basis. I broke it down by each semester. For example, my goal card during my first semester at ETSU simply stated: "I will have a 4.0 GPA by Dec. 23, 1982." And then there was a second goal card, a third, and so on. Four years later, I achieved what appeared to be a big goal, but it was really just an aggregate of little victories all strung together.

Similarly, when I ran for Congress for the first time, I broke down my goal card one step at a time. As a little-known underdog with no rich friends or political connections, the big goal of winning a seat in the U.S. Congress was a bit overwhelming. So, for example, my first goal card simply said: "I will raise $400,000 by August 2000." And later, I wrote a second goal card about making it into the runoff, a third card about winning the nomination, and so on. "Inch by inch, life's a cinch. Yard by yard, life's hard," said author John Bytheway.

In other words, breaking down a larger goal into smaller tasks and accomplishing them one at a time is exactly how any big goal gets achieved. More importantly, the self-confidence you acquire from meeting your early goals is what encourages you to tackle *bigger* and better goals.

For example, achieving my initial goal in college gave me the self-confidence to believe I could win a seat in Congress. If you take away the first achievement, the second one doesn't happen.

Once you are aligned with your purpose, it's a matter of achieving one baby-step goal at a time. You will achieve each step by making a specific goal card, reading it every morning and night, imagining yourself achieving it, trusting your instincts, taking risks, and moving forward with a good-humored attitude despite the naysayers or temporary setbacks.

Can You Imagine Yourself as a Star?

"Imagination is everything. It is the preview to life's coming attractions," said Albert Einstein. It's important to spark your imagination and see yourself achieving your dream goal. Imagine it. Visualize it. Dot Richardson is from my hometown of Orlando. When she was six years old, she viewed the Olympics on TV and saw a pole vaulter from the USA win a gold medal. That night, she began dreaming about being onstage and leaning down to receive a gold medal around her neck.

Twenty-eight years later, at the age of thirty-four, Richardson, the starting shortstop and oldest player on the 1996 US Olympic women's softball team, hit the game-winning home run in the championship game to win the gold medal. She won another gold medal four years later. I had the happy privilege of standing next to her when she told this story to a group of elementary school children in Orlando. Their eyes opened wide when she lifted her gold medals into the air and said, "The power of a dream."

For ten years, I had visualized myself up on the stage on election night, giving a victory speech. When it happened in real life, it was *exactly* how I imagined it would be.

Jim Carrey would look at his $10 million check and visualize famous movie directors wanting to work with him.

Dolly Parton would stand on the porch of her childhood home and sing to the chickens while pretending they were fans attending her show at the Grand Ole Opry.

Jack Canfield and Mark Victor Hansen, authors of the original *Chicken Soup for the Soul,* created a mock-up of the *New York Times* bestsellers list and placed their book in the number-one slot. Within fifteen months, it happened in real life. Four years later, they set a Guinness World Record for having seven books on the *New York Times* bestsellers list at the same time.[14]

Can You Imagine Your Dream Home?

If you have trouble visualizing your goals, a photograph can help keep your conscious and subconscious mind focused on your goals. Don Green, CEO of the Napoleon Hill Foundation, and his wife were looking at an issue of *Better Homes and Gardens* when they noticed a photograph of a beautiful two-story home made from cedar.[15] It had several unique features, including two porches, a long den, and a couple of fireplaces. He wrote the company and found out that the home was located just outside Richmond, Virginia.

Green clipped the picture and put it inside his closet door so he would see it every day. A few weeks later, he happened to be attending a conference in the same town and stopped by to check out the house. He got the name and address of the builder and ordered a set of plans. After the plans arrived, he got someone to build that exact house. He's lived in that same home since 1976.

In 1995, John Assaraf, an entrepreneur and author, saw a beautiful home in *Dream Homes Magazine*. In 2000, he moved into a new home in Southern California. A few weeks later, his five-year-old son came in, noticed some boxes that had been in storage for four years, and asked what was in them. Assaraf said there were vision boards inside. After cutting the box open, the first vision board had photographs of a car he desired and some other items. His son asked about the other vision boards.

Assaraf pulled out the second board and saw something that made him shed a few tears. On that second board was a picture of the house that he had just bought and had been living in for a few weeks. It was not a house like the one he was living in; it was literally the actual house! It was a beautiful 7,000-square-foot home that sat on six acres with spectacular views.

He accidentally bought his dream home. How did he not know? The dream home on the vision board only showed the back of the home; he had never seen a photograph of the front of the home or the front yard with its long driveway.

"Insuring" Your Success

If I had $1 million, I would send a free copy of this book to every newly hired insurance sales agent in the United States. I have seen the three-step formula outlined in this chapter—and advocated by Napoleon Hill—work absolute miracles in the lives of my father, brother, and son. It also was used by W. Clement Stone, an insurance salesman who started out from humble beginnings and built a $2 billion insurance company.

In 1957, Napoleon Hill delivered the commencement speech to the graduating class at Salem College. In this speech, Hill referred to focusing on one thing as a definiteness of purpose. Napoleon Hill told the graduates that out of all the business leaders and presidents he had met over the years, there is no better example of proving that definiteness of purpose pays off than W. Clement Stone.[16] He said:

"Shortly after my book *Think and Grow Rich* was published, Mr. Stone came across a copy of it. At that time, he was earning a modest living as an insurance salesman. That was 1938. As a result of what my book said about the need to choose a definite goal in life, Mr. Stone took a notebook from his pocket and wrote the following words: 'My goal in life is this: By 1956 I will be president at the biggest, exclusive, old-line legal reserve, health, and accident insurance company in the world.'

"Mr. Stone signed his name to this and began reading it over to himself daily until it was seared into his consciousness. And because he knew what he wanted, he was able to recognize opportunity when it came his way. When the chance came for him to acquire the Combined Insurance Company of America, he was able to act with swift determination toward accomplishing his goal. And through his energy, the firm has now become what he determined it would be: the biggest exclusive accident and health firm in the world."[17]

After achieving great success, Stone donated his time and talent to helping others become successful and donated $275 million of his fortune to charitable organizations.

When I met my father for the first time when I was fourteen years old, he gave me a paperback copy of his favorite book, *Think and Grow Rich,* and told me his story. Dad had been a stockbroker at a big Wall Street firm. It didn't go well. One of the stars in the office noticed that my dad was struggling. As a tip, the guy suggested that Dad read *Think and Grow Rich.* It didn't help. He wasn't ready. He didn't take action, and his heart wasn't into being a stockbroker. The book sat on a shelf, gathering dust.

Many years later, Dad started a new endeavor. He opened a State Farm Insurance agency on Long Island, New York. This time, he was ready. As an experiment, he decided to apply the techniques he learned about in *Think and Grow Rich.* He made a goal card. He read it every morning and night. And he visualized himself achieving it.

My dad's goal was to sell more fire insurance policies than anyone in New York history. And he did it. Next, he set a goal to sell more fire policies than anyone in the northeastern United States. He did that, too. He went on to become one of the top eighteen State Farm agents in the country in fire insurance.

Think and Grow Rich had changed my dad's life; now he hoped it would change mine, too. I was inspired by his story and read it six times. I then set some big goals that came true, including graduating first in my class in college, going to Vanderbilt Law School, and getting elected to Congress. Dad had become very successful selling insurance and generously picked up the steep tab for Vanderbilt.

Dad also passed along *Think and Grow Rich* to my youngest brother, Jarret Orenstein. After graduating from college, Jarret had tried various jobs, including working as a production assistant on movies starring Jennifer Lopez and Jake Gyllenhaal. But, like Dad, he eventually found his niche selling insurance and opened up his own State Farm Insurance agency in Great Neck, Long Island. Using the same three-step formula in this chapter, Jarret is now ranked in the top 1 percent in selling automobile insurance out of 19,000 State Farm agents.

My son, Nick Keller, is also in the insurance business. Although he was a bright kid, his academic record in college wasn't the best. He moved back to Orlando and got a job at a hotel as a bellboy and valet parking attendant. I had given him a copy of *Think and Grow Rich* many years earlier, but he wasn't ready for it and didn't read it. It sat around gathering dust.

And then Nick landed a new job selling health insurance. This time, he was ready for it and read it. My son set a goal to sell over $1 million in health insurance by the end of his first year. And he did it. He then set a bigger goal to sell more than $100,000 per week and did that, too. He went on to open the Chicago office for his company and has a big team of agents working for him. Nick constantly keeps his goals top of mind by making them the "wallpaper" on his iPhone. By using the world's most powerful goal-setting formula, he went from parking cars and carrying luggage to driving a Mercedes and living in a beautiful home. You can, too—if that's your goal.

The insurance business is the great equalizer. It's tailor-made for people who are open to setting goals and to using this powerful three-step formula to achieve them. I would love to see every newly hired insurance agent use these same principles to experience the same abundant life enjoyed by my father, brother, and son.

You know your gift. You know your goal. Now you need to know and trust your internal GPS system to guide you.

TAKEAWAY

Write down your specific goal (including a date) on a three-inch by five-inch card. Read it every morning and night. See and feel yourself "up on the stage" having already achieved it.

CHAPTER 3
Trust Your Intuition

*"Have the courage to follow your heart and intuition.
They somehow already know what you
truly want to become."*
—Steve Jobs

When we want to align with our highest truths, life will flood us with insights and signs so we are clear about these decisions. The insights are "intuition." The signs are "coincidences."

By analogy, imagine your goal is to drive to Disney World in Orlando. The destination is your goal. The vehicle to get you there is your gift. The GPS on board is your intuition. The signs along the way are coincidences. The first two chapters were about your gifts and goals. This chapter is about your guidance system (i.e., intuition and coincidences) to keep you on track.

Intuition: Our Internal Guidance System

Intuition is your internal GPS system. It provides you with a gut feeling, or inner voice, telling you something is good or bad. "Trust instinct to the end, though you can render no reason," wrote Ralph Waldo Emerson.

Successful people trust their intuition. You should, too. "Every right decision I've ever made has come from my gut. And every wrong decision I've made was a result of me not listening to the greater voice of myself," said Oprah Winfrey.[18]

Trusting my instincts has made all the difference in my life. My instincts told me to become a lawyer/politician instead of a doctor, to run for Congress as an underdog, and to stay in the race despite a party leader asking me to quit.

Trust your instincts no matter how unconventional or unpopular they seem. Your intuition is more powerful than anyone's advice. Whether you call it a gut feeling, intuition, or instinct, it's important to listen to it, trust it, and act on it.

Connecting Through Coincidences

"Coincidence is God's way of remaining anonymous," said Albert Einstein. The famed psychologist Carl Jung believed that coincidences are meaningful events, and he referred to them as "synchronicity."

I, too, have come to believe that so-called "coincidences" are often meaningful events that can help keep you on your true path. We are all connected. Ever notice how the right people and events come into your life at just the right time?

Was it just a coincidence that I was sipping a beer at a Poconos pub and asking for a sign about whether I should become a doctor or a politician when I noticed a poster on the wall for a *politician's* barbecue the next day?

Was it just a coincidence that weeks after I set a fundraising goal of $400,000, I was invited to give a five-minute talk to a group of CEOs and business leaders in DC that culminated in them spending exactly $400,000 to support me?

Was it just a coincidence that in law school, I mailed a note to my dad on *November 7, 1990,* stating, "I plan on busting my ass to get elected to Congress," and ten years later to the exact date, on *November 7, 2000,* I won a seat in Congress?

Pay attention to coincidences. They are signs to help keep you on your true path. The right people, hunches, and things will appear in your life *when you are ready* for them.

If you "randomly" bump into someone on *three* occasions, then really pay attention—the Universe is whispering to you. For example, my amazing wife, Lori, and I "met" at the *third* event we both attended over a year and a half. All three events were receptions for mutual friends seeking public office. I didn't remember meeting her at the first two events. I wasn't ready. It was only at the *third* event— when we were both single—that Lori appeared in my life in a big way. The date was February 28. We got married exactly one year later to the date.

Marrying Lori was one of the happiest days of my life.

The "Gut Feeling" Worth a Billion Dollars[19]

Jamie Kern Lima started a makeup company out of her living room. Since her twenties, she had battled the skin condition rosacea, which left red blotches on her face. After graduating with an MBA from Columbia, she developed a product to help other women with similar skin problems.

Kern Lima had a clear vision, a good product, and a willingness to work one-hundred-hour weeks without pay. Still, after three years, she had little to show for her efforts. Her company was only selling two to three units of concealer a day off her website, and she was down to less than $1,000 in the bank.

And then Kern Lima caught a small break. QVC, the home shopping network, gave her a one-time-only chance to sell her product on-air during a brief segment. There was a catch. She had to sell 6,000 units of concealer within ten minutes. If not, she'd have to absorb the cost of the 6,000 units and would never be invited back. It was a big risk.

Before the big day, she consulted several experts who specialized in selling products on TV. The "logical" advice of all the experts was for her to demonstrate the use of the makeup product on beautiful models in their early twenties with perfect skin.

In contrast, Kern Lima's intuition told her to go on camera without any makeup (exposing her red facial blotches to millions of TV viewers) and apply the product to herself. Although her approach was unconventional, she felt it would show regular women that the product was easy to use and would help them look beautiful, too.

The future of the company was at stake. Should she go with her gut feeling or follow experts' advice? She went with her gut and demonstrated the product on herself. And then, with only seconds remaining of the ten-minute segment, a "sold out" sign popped up on the TV screen, indicating that all 6,000 units had been sold. She was invited back to QVC many times and would eventually do over 200 QVC appearances in one year.

The success of Kern Lima's company caught the attention of L'Oréal, the world's largest beauty and makeup company. L'Oréal bought the company for over a *billion* dollars in a cash deal.

In her memoir, *Believe It,* Jamie Kern Lima wrote: "Making the decision to trust my gut when literally everything was on the line opened every other door afterward. That single moment was in big part responsible for turning a dream that I started in my living room into a billion-dollar company. I truly believe our own gut instinct is one of our greatest superpowers."[20]

"Ivy League Redneck"

Kern Lima is not the only Ivy League MBA grad with the courage to trust her intuition. I've never met anyone better at trusting her intuition than my wife, Lori Spivey Keller. Many years ago, Lori wrote a poem called "Ivy League Redneck" in reference to herself. It's a funny and fitting description.

Lori came from a modest blue-collar and rural background. She worked on her family's palm tree farm, cooked fried squirrel for dinner, and was a member of the 4-H agricultural club. One summer, when she was thirteen, her 4-H club sponsored a trip to the University of Florida. Walking through UF's student union building, Lori noticed photographs on the wall of students who belonged to UF's prestigious Hall of Fame. She dreamed about becoming a Gator and seeing her photograph on the wall as well.

Lori attended high school in a lower-income area where only a small percentage of the students went to college, but she had good grades and was accepted to UF. Money was tight, and many people, including her guidance counselor, strongly encouraged her to play it safe, live at home for a couple of years, and attend the local community college because "the first two years are the same anyway."

Should she play it safe or follow her heart? Lori followed her heart and went to UF. She made ends meet by landing a part-time job and cobbling together a series of smaller scholarships to supplement help from her family.

Four years later, Lori was Homecoming Queen, graduated as the Outstanding Female Leader, and was inducted into the UF Hall of Fame. The significance to Lori wasn't the accomplishments. Rather, it was the life lesson that we should *trust our intuition*. She had also unknowingly *visualized* these achievements from the time she was thirteen years old. (It's a good idea for you to take a moment and reread the visualization instructions included in the powerful three-step formula described in Chapter 2, along with the explanation provided in that chapter for why these visualizations work.)

This lesson would soon come in handy. After graduating from UF, Lori landed a great job in Nashville with Procter & Gamble—a huge company that sells products like Tide, Pantene, and Crest toothpaste.

Her career was off to a strong start. She had a fantastic job with a great salary, health insurance, and a company car. Best of all, after working there for nearly four years, Lori was offered a promotion to a brand-management position at Procter & Gamble's headquarters in Cincinnati. It's the path to CEO and a role that many people covet.

It was a fork in the road. Her *logical* mind told her to play it safe and take the lucrative promotion offered by Procter & Gamble, but her *intuition* told her to go abroad and gain international experience. She didn't know why she felt this way. After all, no one in her family even had a passport, and if they went on vacation, they never went more than a car ride away.

Once again, she followed her heart. Lori quit her job and moved to Amsterdam, even though she didn't have a job lined up ahead of time. Her family and many friends thought she was nuts for giving up a great job, health insurance, and a company car. But Lori learned to speak Dutch, quickly landed an international marketing position, and bought a bike to get around town.

While living in Amsterdam, a friend who worked for a small Dutch startup called TomTom asked Lori if they could record her voice for this new voice navigation product they were developing called the TomTom GPS Navigation system. Although Lori had never done voice work in her life, she thought it would be fun and said yes.

Much to her surprise, the "Lori voice" became TomTom's default voice for the English language around the world in millions of automobiles. It's quite the irony being married to Lori. Her "inner voice" (and internal GPS) guides her decision-making, while her "outer voice" (and literal GPS) tells me how to drive!

The company went on to generate over a billion dollars a year in revenue. For her voice work, Lori was paid only $350 by TomTom. Her CPA called her "dum-dum." Lori figured she had a lot to learn about business.

After nearly four years of living in Amsterdam, Lori was ready for the next chapter of her life, and she applied to Harvard Business School. The essay from her Harvard application stood out. They were impressed by her unique experiences abroad and how she boldly left a safe job to gain an international perspective. Lori got accepted to Harvard and received her MBA degree two years later. She was now officially an "Ivy League redneck."

After Harvard, Lori worked as a business consultant at the prestigious Boston Consulting Group for ten years, became an executive at a Fortune 500 company, and created a nonprofit charity that increases access to healthcare in Africa.

Lori speaks to young people about the importance of trusting your intuition. For example, in a speech at the annual *Young Leaders Conference* (which she founded) for high school students held at UF, Lori said:

> "We've all experienced it: We have to make a choice, and one of the options seems logical, reasonable, safe, fits with expectations, and might be the natural next step. The other option doesn't seem to be as logical or may not be the next standard step in your career or life, but it 'feels' right—our instinct, heart, gut, God, the Universe, is telling us, screaming at us, to take the less logical path. I've been faced with this scenario several times and in different circumstances have made both choices—the safe choice my brain told me to make and the illogical choice my heart told me to take. Ultimately, I never regretted following my heart—every single time it turned out to be the right decision. The seemingly logical choices were the ones that ended up not working out as well as I expected them to."

The "Gut Feeling" That Foiled Osama Bin Laden—Twice[21]

I'll close this chapter with a little-known story about a humble man who changed the world by trusting his intuition.

On August 4, 2001, Mohammed al-Qahtani, a twenty-six-year-old Saudi man traveling alone, arrived at Orlando International

Airport via a Virgin Atlantic flight. I know this airport well because I
live in Orlando and would fly in and out of it every week.

In this case, because the young man could not speak English—
and needed help filling out his entry form—the standard protocol
required that he be interviewed by an inspector from the Immigration
and Naturalization Service (INS).

José Meléndez-Pérez was one of the immigration inspectors on
duty that day. At approximately 5:35 PM, Meléndez-Pérez walked over
to meet Qahtani and invited Qahtani to follow him into an inspec-
tion room, which was a ten-by-ten-foot room with a desk, computer,
and telephone. Meléndez-Pérez arranged for an Arabic interpreter to
appear by telephone to assist in the interview.

Objectively, everything looked just fine. Qahtani's passport docu-
ments were in order, and the computer background check came back
all clear. However, during the interview, it seemed odd to Meléndez-
Pérez that Qahtani did not have a return airline ticket or a hotel res-
ervation. Also, Qahtani displayed a hostile attitude—which included
aggressive finger-pointing—during what should have been a quick,
easy, and routine interview.

"I had a 'gut feeling' that something wasn't right," Meléndez-Pérez
said. "I felt a bone-chilling cold affect. The bottom line is, he gave me
the creeps." The immigration inspector knew something was off, but
he didn't know why. Therefore, even though Qahtani's passport and
background check were normal, Meléndez-Pérez trusted his instincts
and blocked Qahtani from entering the United States.

Fast forward one month later to Tuesday, September 11, 2001. I
was in Washington because the United States Congress was back in
session. I began the morning by walking from my Capitol Hill apartment to my office, located a few blocks away. At around 8:30 AM, I
arrived at my Capitol Hill office to the smell of Dunkin' Donuts and

freshly brewed coffee. I was meeting with a sheriff who was in town to testify at a congressional hearing later that day in favor of legislation I drafted called the "No Frills Prison Act." I was a freshman and excited about attending the hearing.

My meeting with the sheriff was cut short after the first two planes struck the World Trade Center. After the third plane crashed into the Pentagon, we realized we could be the next target. There began the chaos. Capitol Hill police officers began running into the congressional offices and shouting, "Everybody out! Everybody out!"

As I exited the building, I saw thick black smoke billowing out of the Pentagon. I began walking back to my Capitol Hill apartment. En route, I heard the sonic booms from fighter jets as they scrambled to the airspace above us, and I noticed a TV camera crew setting up to get a shot of the Capitol dome—presumably to have video footage in case a plane struck the dome. I wondered, *When will this end?*

The end came minutes later when the fourth plane, United Airlines Flight 93, crashed into a field in Shanksville, Pennsylvania, at 10:03 AM, only twenty minutes flying time from Washington, DC. Significantly, United Flight 93 was the *only* one of the four hijacked planes on 9/11 that did not reach its intended destination—which was the US Capitol building, according to Khalid Sheikh Mohammed (the mastermind of the 9/11 attacks)—and it was also the only plane with four (not five) hijackers. They were shorthanded.

The reason why the Flight 93 hijackers were shorthanded was that José Meléndez-Pérez had blocked Qahtani from entering the country. This thwarted Qahtani's deadly mission to provide "muscle" as the fifth hijacker aboard United Flight 93. The understaffed hijackers were unable to fend off the passengers' courageous revolt—which began with the words from passenger Todd Beamer, "Let's roll." Together, Meléndez-Pérez and the Flight 93 heroes may have saved hundreds of lives, including mine, and prevented the virtual decapitation of the Capitol dome.

I paid tribute to my constituent, José Meléndez-Pérez, in a televised speech given on the floor of the U.S. House of Representatives. I concluded my remarks, as published in the *Congressional Record,* by saying, "Every time he has been asked about his role in stopping the twentieth hijacker, Mr. Meléndez-Pérez always says, 'I was just doing my job.' Well, Mr. Meléndez-Pérez, I say to you, 'Job well done.'"

Astonishingly, the story doesn't end there. Qahtani, the twentieth hijacker, was later captured along the Afghanistan-Pakistan border and sent to Guantanamo Bay, where he became the first person to identify bin Laden's trusted courier. This was the all-important clue that ultimately helped the CIA and SEAL Team Six follow the breadcrumbs to Osama bin Laden's compound in Pakistan, where he and the courier had been living for about five years.

Meléndez-Pérez had foiled bin Laden a second time.

"If Qahtani had been allowed entry, he would have been aboard United Flight 93, where his added muscle might have kept resisting passengers at bay for the twenty additional minutes the flight needed to reach its target, the US Capitol. And if Qahtani had died on Flight 93, we wouldn't have learned the name of bin Laden's courier from him," said Michael Smerconish, the CNN television host and author of *Instinct: The Man Who Stopped the 20th Hijacker.*[22]

Meléndez-Pérez listened to his gut feeling, trusted it, and acted on it. You should, too. Trusting your intuition is a "little thing" that can change your life . . . *and maybe the world.*

TAKEAWAY

Trust your intuition no matter how unconventional or
unpopular your choice seems.

CHAPTER 4
Take Risks

"You can fail at what you don't want, so you might as well take a chance on doing what you love."
—Jim Carrey

Every successful person has taken risks. What holds many of us back from taking risks is *fear*. When I talk about taking risks, I'm not talking about strapping yourself into a rocket motorcycle—like the daredevil Evel Knievel did—and jumping the Snake River Canyon. I'm talking about taking educated, baby-step risks that are aligned with your purpose.

Still, taking chances can be scary. What if people think you're crazy? What if you get rejected? What if your heart gets broken? What if you fail? Listen, I get that it's scary out there. I've been humiliated. I've been beaten. I've been shot at. And that's just from my wife after the last boys' weekend away.

In all seriousness, it is true that all of these things are possible, at least temporarily. But it is also true that you've got to take chances to fulfill your mission in life. You've got to take chances to feel alive. You've got to take chances to experience true love.

What if It All Goes Right?

Many years ago, there was a TV show called *Nashville Star*. It featured up-and-coming country singers who competed for the chance to win a record deal, sort of a country music version of *American Idol*. I tuned in one night and was moved when the contest winner, Melissa Lawson, sang "What if It All Goes Right?", a beautiful song written by Shaye Smith, Tania Hancheroff, and Tammy Hyler. The song's powerful message rang true to me. Instead of worrying about all the things that could go wrong, why not ask yourself, *What if it all goes right?* What if the stars align? What if good luck is on your side? What if you "chased the bears" and it changes your whole life?

The question "What if it all goes right?" is powerful, in part, because it is the exact opposite of fear. Yes, you might temporarily stumble, but then again, you might fly. But how do you know? Here is the closest guarantee I can give you: The secret is alignment. *If you are aligned with your purpose and use your gifts to serve the greater good, then you will still stumble from time to time and experience temporary setbacks, but you will never fail on any permanent basis.* "When your life is on course with its purpose, you are at your most powerful. And though you may stumble, you will not fail," said Oprah Winfrey.

Steve Harvey: He Got the Gold Star After All

Eighteenth-century Irish poet Oliver Goldsmith wrote, "You can preach a better sermon with your life than with your lips." Steve

Harvey epitomizes Goldsmith's insight. Harvey is a comedian, best-selling author, and Emmy Award-winning TV game show host of *Family Feud*. He is also, in my humble opinion, the most talented inspirational speaker in the world. He combines the humor of Dave Chappelle, the optimism of Joel Osteen, and the wisdom gleaned from his own life experiences to inspire people to use their gifts and take risks (he calls it "jumping") in the direction of their dreams.

Harvey knew he was funny since childhood but suffered from a serious stuttering problem that made it difficult for him to talk until age fifteen. There were three key turning points in his life.[23]

First, when he was in sixth grade, his teacher asked everyone in the class to write down on a piece of paper what they want to be when they grow up. Harvey wrote, "I want to be on TV." The teacher asked him to come up to the front of the class. He thought he was going to get a gold star, but instead, she humiliated him. She asked him if he knew anybody in his family, school, or neighborhood who had ever been on TV. She thought his goal was unrealistic. Other kids said they hoped to be firemen, policemen, or doctors.

By the time he got home, his teacher had already spoken with his mom, who was also concerned. However, to his credit, Harvey's father said, "Well, what's wrong with that?" His father told him to read that piece of paper every morning when he woke up and every night before he went to bed, and that is just what Harvey did for the next ten years. As he read the note twice a day, he imagined himself on TV.[24] (Reread the secret formula in Chapter 2 and you'll see that Harvey was applying the same powerful technique.)

The second key turning point happened when Harvey was twenty-seven years old and won an amateur-night comedy contest. The prize was fifty dollars. Harvey had been kicked out of college for bad grades and had a series of jobs before finally getting some stability as an insurance salesman. However, this event made him feel like he finally figured out what he was meant to do. "I was born tonight," Harvey told a friend. He quit his insurance job the next day.

It was a rough start. As he pursued his dream, he was homeless for three years and lived out of his car while driving around the country to perform at comedy clubs. The first year doing comedy, he only made $3,500, the second year $5,000, and the third year $6,800. His marriage fell apart, too.

Harvey was on the verge of quitting just before the third turning point.[25] He got a phone message from a man named Chuck Sutton, asking if he was available that Sunday night to perform on the *Showtime at the Apollo* TV variety show filmed in Harlem, New York.

Harvey was thrilled and excited to do it, but he was in Florida and didn't have enough money to get there. Then he got a second message from a Florida comedy club owner, who offered him a gig that paid him enough money to buy a plane ticket to New York. He made it to the Apollo, did extremely well, and got a standing ovation. It was his first television appearance.

Shortly thereafter, Sutton offered Harvey a permanent job as host of *Showtime at the Apollo*, and he's been on TV ever since.[26] At one point, he hosted the *Family Feud* TV game show, the *Steve Harvey* talk show, and a nationally syndicated radio show—all at the same time. He also became a number-one *New York Times* bestselling author, won six Emmy Awards, has a reported net worth of $200 million, a Star on the Hollywood Walk of Fame, and a movie based on his book made $100 million.[27]

Remember that sixth-grade teacher who made fun of Harvey's dream to be on TV? Harvey said that he sent her a flat-screen TV every Christmas because "I want to make sure she can see me."[28]

Colonel Sanders: It's Never Too Late

It is never too late to start a business, go back to school, or use your gifts. You can still be what you wish to be. Colonel Harland Sanders was sixty-two when he opened his first Kentucky Fried Chicken.[29] Before that, the Colonel had lots of jobs—and setbacks.

He tried everything. He worked as a farmhand, streetcar conductor, steamboat ferry operator, country lawyer, insurance salesman, and gas station attendant. The Colonel thought he finally found his niche when he opened the Sanders Café in Corbin, Kentucky. Unfortunately, a new highway was built that bypassed the town of Corbin, and Sanders was forced to close his doors. By his mid-sixties, the Colonel found himself out of money and living on his $105 a month Social Security check.

But there was one positive thing. The Colonel had figured out that his gift was making "Finger lickin' good" fried chicken, and he perfected his secret recipe of eleven herbs and spices while working at Sanders Café. He had an idea. What if he began touring the country and trying to talk restaurant owners into converting their establishments into Kentucky Fried Chicken franchises? His proposal was simple. He would sell them the secret recipe, and in return, they'd pay him a nickel for each piece of chicken sold. The idea took off. He opened his first KFC franchise in Utah, landed a few more in Indiana and Ohio, and today there are 25,000 KFC restaurants globally in 146 countries. It's the world's second-largest restaurant chain. The Colonel passed away at age ninety in 1980, but his iconic image with the white mustache, goatee, and double-breasted suit is still world-famous and appears on every bucket of chicken and KFC sign.

Dave the Cook[30]

Dave started working at the Hobby House restaurant in Fort Wayne, Indiana, as a busboy at age fifteen. He was working long hours at the restaurant and dropped out of high school after tenth grade. Dave's boss, restaurant owner Phil Clauss, was impressed with Dave's strong work ethic and promoted him to short-order cook.

By his twenties, Dave had been promoted again to head cook and assistant manager of the Hobby House restaurant, he had married one of the waitresses, and they had two kids. Dave was working twelve-hour days but was only making $75 a week. He was constantly strapped and in need of more money. He thought there had to be a golden egg. But when the opportunity came, it appeared in a different form than he expected.

One day, a sixty-five-year-old man driving a white Cadillac pulled up to the Hobby House restaurant. He made quite the entrance as he walked in unannounced through the front doors of the restaurant. He looked like a Southern gentleman with his white mustache, white goatee, and gold-tipped cane. It was none other than the Colonel himself.

The Colonel asked to speak with a manager. Dave later described that day: "We sat down over a cup of coffee, and he talked to me like an old friend. I've never met a better salesman. When he left, I had a sense this man was going to change my life."

Dave's boss ultimately decided to convert his Fort Wayne, Indiana, restaurant into a Kentucky Fried Chicken franchise, and he also bought four KFC franchises in Columbus, Ohio. The Indiana store managed by Dave was a huge success, but the four Columbus stores were failures. Clauss offered Dave a 40 percent ownership share if he would move to Columbus and turn the stores around.

It was a huge risk for Dave. The four stores had already lost $250,000, his wife would have to give up friends and family in Indiana, and their family had expanded to five children. Clauss said, "I know it's a long shot, Dave, but I think you can do it."

Dave's intuition told him to do it. With forty bucks in his pocket, Dave loaded the family in the car and moved to Columbus. It didn't mean that Dave wasn't scared. He said:

"When Phil Clauss offered me four bankrupt KFC stores, although I knew it was an opportunity, deep down I was afraid, and there were times when I got depressed. When that happened, instead of defeating myself, I made an effort to change my thoughts. I forced myself to believe that I could do it, and then went back to working hard and giving it 150 percent . . . The trick is never to let yourself wallow in being unhappy."

Staying positive allowed his creative juices to flow. For example, it was Dave who created the rotating KFC chicken bucket sign that was eventually used by all the KFC stores across the country. Dave also is the one who wisely urged Colonel Sanders to appear in more TV commercials to promote the brand.

It worked. A few years later, Dave turned the four stores around and sold his stake in the company for $1.5 million. He was a millionaire at age thirty-five, virtually unheard of back in the sixties.

A year later, Dave parlayed that investment into opening his own restaurant. Dave had always loved hamburgers more than chicken. In a world of round hamburgers, Dave decided to do something different and sell square hamburgers. He also wanted to have a milkshake that was so thick you'd need a spoon to eat it instead of a straw. Also, taking his own advice to Colonel Sanders, Dave personally appeared in the restaurant's television ads.

His name is Dave Thomas. He named the restaurant after his daughter, Wendy. Today, Wendy's is the world's third-largest hamburger restaurant chain, with more than 6,700 locations. In his autobiography, *Dave's Way*, Thomas wrote:

"Your fears and self-doubts are your personal traps. You may say, 'I've never done it before, how do I know I can do it?' Well, you don't know. There are never any guarantees, but there are also no rewards without risk. Talk positively to yourself because your own negative thoughts will hold you back more than any other person will."

After his great success as a restaurateur, Dave Thomas went back to school and earned his high school diploma (GED) at age sixty-one. His classmates voted him Most Likely to Succeed and elected him Prom King. After Thomas passed away in 2002, he was posthumously awarded the Presidential Medal of Freedom, America's highest civilian honor, by President George W. Bush.

Colonel Harland Sanders and Dave Thomas both used their gifts, trusted their intuition, and took risks. In an interview with *POV Magazine*, Dave Thomas was asked, "What kind of advice would you give to today's twenty-five-year-olds?" He replied, "You've got to like what you do. Be persistent. Keep focused. And have fun doing it."[31]

It's interesting, but not totally surprising, how Colonel Sanders and Dave Thomas are connected. A seemingly "chance meeting" between the two men at that little restaurant in Fort Wayne, Indiana, would change the world. We are all connected. Little did I know, as a young man, that my story would connect as well.

Wendy's and Me

I was a fifteen-year-old high school student looking to earn money to buy my first car. The local Wendy's was only three blocks from my home. I got hired and rode my bike to the restaurant for my first day of work. The manager handed me a light blue-and-white striped shirt, matching cabbie-style hat, and my own name tag with "Ric" in red letters.

After that, he walked me up to the front of the grill. I never saw him again. Apparently, my entry-level training apprenticeship had fallen through the management cracks. Nobody told me how to work the deep fryers, grills, or cash register.

To make the best of it, I carefully watched how the other employees did things. I kept opening white bags of frozen french fries and placing them into the deep-fryer baskets. I held the silver spatula in my right hand and flipped each burger individually like a perfectionist. Unbeknownst to me, I was too slow.

The second day would be more of the same. No training. But one coworker did give me an "insider tip"—any burgers that were left over after being cooked should be cut up and placed into the pot of chili. Check. I did it. So far, so good . . . at least I thought.

On my third (and final) day, I noticed a very attractive lady assistant manager on duty. She had auburn hair and appeared to be in her mid-twenties. I was an optimistic, red-blooded teenager with a crush.

During the shift, the pretty manager walked behind me and whispered in my ear—as her hand slowly grazed across my lower back—"Drop by my office after your shift is over." I felt excited. After my shift, I walked over and knocked on the cute manager's door.

"Hi Ric, come on in. Close the door," she said. I thought to myself, *This is going to be awesome*—but my fantasy would quickly melt faster than a chocolate Frosty on a hot summer day in Florida.

"Ric, this is the part of the job that I hate the most," she began. "I'm so sorry. But we've got to let you go. *You just don't have what it takes to make it in fast food*," she said.

It was humiliating. I felt like a loser. *Am I not good enough for Wendy's or the cute girl?* There are many ironic twists to this story. I had no way of knowing it at the time, but twenty-five years later, Wendy's would become one of my biggest campaign donors. Wendy's political contributions of $12,500 to my congressional campaigns translate to about $1,000 for each hour I worked there. I think that makes me the world's highest-paid fast-food reject.

Bouncing Back

After getting fired, I hopped on my bike and started to pedal the "ride of shame" back home. But instead of giving up, I made a turn and pedaled over to a new restaurant called Wag's. It was a restaurant chain owned by Walgreens back in the eighties, and it was similar to Denny's. It has since gone out of business. I filled out a Wag's job application and got hired as a dishwasher. The cooks made a dollar more per hour than dishwashers, so I worked hard and set a goal to get promoted to cook. I noticed the more talented breakfast cooks at Wag's had a cool way of cracking the eggs with one hand and then later flipping the eggs in the air with the frying pan.

I had my mom buy dozens and dozens of eggs so I could practice every night, learning how to crack the eggs with one hand and flip them, too. One year later, at age sixteen, there was an opening for a short-order cook. I showed the manager my skills and got the promotion. The higher-paying job enabled me to buy my dream car—a blue convertible MG Midget. The sting of the Wendy's rejection was over.

This brings up the second ironic twist. In his book, Wendy's founder Dave Thomas wrote, "Don't be discouraged if an early job doesn't work out. I was fired from or quit my first six jobs." The first job Dave got fired from was at the Walgreens restaurant, and then he later started Wendy's. The first job I got fired from was at Wendy's, and I later got a job at Walgreens restaurant.

Lessons from Failure

I learned three valuable life lessons from my "failure" of getting fired by Wendy's. The first lesson is that setbacks are only temporary. The comeback (Wag's) was stronger than the setback (Wendy's). I got more money, had more fun, swapped out the silly Wendy's cabbie hat for a cool Wag's chef's hat, and switched from a BMX bike to a sports car.

The second lesson is don't hold grudges. Wendy's fired me, but later they helped me more than anybody. Despite being let go, I stayed positive about my feelings toward Wendy's. I deeply admired Dave Thomas, plus nobody loves a Wendy's double cheeseburger and Frosty more than me. This had solid practical applications that helped me be a better congressman. There are no permanent friends and no permanent enemies, especially in Washington. For example, in Congress, I would never get mad at a colleague on the other side of the aisle for voting against my tax bill, because later he would be the one who helped me the most on my bill to increase Pell Grants. Civility, I learned, is the watchword.

The third lesson is to always bring my A game to the job. I never wanted to get fired again. For example, while I was a cook at Wag's, the local media outlets had someone called "the mystery diner" who would go around to restaurants in Orlando and give food reviews. I pretended that every single order of food I made was personally being reviewed by the mystery diner. I have no idea whether he ever came to Wag's during the three years I worked there.

No Salad for Caesar

I also had no idea that one day I'd play a positive role in helping Wendy's and KFC in Congress. The "connection" theme continues. It's a bizarre tale.

Caesar Barber, age fifty-six, was a maintenance worker from the Bronx who weighed 272 pounds. He filed the first-ever class-action lawsuit against McDonald's, Burger King, Wendy's, and KFC in July 2002. He blamed the restaurants for his obesity. Barber—who ate fast-food four to five times a week even after suffering two heart attacks—told ABC's *Good Morning America*, "They never explained to me what I was eating."[32]

In an interview with *60 Minutes*, he said:

Barber: "I want compensation for pain and suffering."

60 Minutes: "How much money do you want?"

Barber: "Maybe $1 million. That's not a lot of money now."

Caesar Barber wanted the money, not the salad.

Other "obesity suits" followed. The American public wasn't swayed by these lawsuits. A Gallup Poll indicated that nine out of ten Americans opposed holding the fast-food industry legally responsible for diet-related health. Richard Simmons, the celebrity health guru, wasn't a fan either. He said, "These people who bring these suits don't need a lawyer, they need a psychiatrist."

It was no joke to the restaurant industry, the country's largest private-sector provider of jobs. On February 10, 2003, *Fortune* magazine's cover asked, "Is Fat the Next Tobacco?" and subtitled: "The war over obesity will be fought in the courts. That's bad news for Big Food."

At the time, I was on the House Judiciary Committee. I thought *enough is enough*. I understood weight struggles as well as anybody. But whatever happened to personal responsibility? In early 2003, I authored legislation called the Personal Responsibility in Food Consumption Act, nicknamed the "cheeseburger bill" by the media, which blocked frivolous obesity-related lawsuits against restaurants and food producers.

The "heavy-hitters" supported the "cheeseburger bill." The White House issued a press release endorsing the bill. Senator Mitch McConnell (R-KY) subsequently filed the companion bill in the Senate— called the Common Sense in Food Consumption Act.

To my surprise, the legislation sparked a national debate. The *New York Times, Washington Post*, and *Associated Press* wrote articles about it, and Neil Cavuto of *Fox News Channel* brought me on his show to discuss the bill on national television:

Cavuto: "Congressman, you said enough is enough?"[33]

Me: "Absolutely. The gist of this legislation is that there should be common sense in the food court, not blaming other people in a legal court whenever there's an excessive consumption of fast food . . . I think most people have enough common sense to realize, if you eat an unlimited amount of cheeseburgers and milkshakes and super-size fries and chocolate sundaes, it may lead to obesity."

Cavuto: "You're saying we are responsible for our own actions?"

Me: "I think we've got to get back to the principles of freedom of choice, common sense, and personal responsibility, and get away from this culture where everybody plays the victim and tries to blame others for their problems."

There would be no money (or salad) for Caesar Barber. The U.S. House of Representatives ultimately approved my bill by a 306 to 120 vote on October 19, 2005, and CNN reported, "Cheeseburger bill takes a bite out of lawsuits." And the court threw out Barber's suit.

This leads me to tell you the third ironic thing about this story. I missed the vote on my own bill. That was *my* overweight period, and I was hospitalized for suspected cardiac arrhythmia.

The bill would have been overwhelmingly approved by the Senate, too, but it wasn't called up for a vote. Two interesting things happened after I filed the cheeseburger bill.

First, twenty-six states ended up passing their own cheeseburger bills. The cheeseburger bills curbed litigation and waistlines. For example, the University of Chicago's *Journal of Law and Economics* published a study by Vanderbilt researchers called, "Do Cheeseburger Bills Work? Effect of Tort Reform for Fast Food," which found that people who lived in states with cheeseburger bills reported "significantly increased healthy food consumption as measured by the number of servings of fruits and vegetables consumed per day."[34]

Second, it started a national conversation that ultimately led to restaurants disclosing the calorie counts on their menus and fast-food chains voluntarily offering more healthful menu options. The combination of these actions virtually immunized restaurants from future suits.

"Lock Up" in the Hamburger Jail

Some opponents speculated that I championed the cheeseburger bill because of campaign contributions. The argument didn't carry much weight. The other side of the issue was far more lucrative. The trial lawyers out-contributed McDonald's 53-to-1—the trial lawyers' PAC gave $2.2 million in political contributions to candidates, compared to McDonald's PAC's donations of $41,000.[35]

The truth, however, never got in the way of political attack ads, which would be the fourth ironic outcome of this saga.

One day, I was driving down the road with two of my young daughters, Kate and Kaylee, sitting in the back seat. Out of the blue, they asked me several rapid-fire questions before I could even answer:

Kate: "Dad, why did you rob Wendy's and KFC?"

Kaylee: "And you robbed McDonald's, Burger King, and Pizza Hut, too!"

Kate: "Did you go to prison?"

Kaylee: "Yeah, how long were you in prison?"

Kate: "Tell the truth!"

Kaylee: "We know everything! We saw it on YouTube."

Me: "What the heck are you talking about?"

Kaylee: "It said something like, 'Write Congressman Ric Keller and ask him why he took money from McDonald's, Wendy's, Burger King, Pizza Hut, and Kentucky Fried Chicken.'"

Me (laughing): "Girls, that's not about me robbing restaurants. It is just a silly political attack ad. It was referring to political contributions from restaurants' political action committees to my congressional campaign committee."

Kate (skeptical): "Sure. Sure it is, Dad."

Kaylee (also skeptical): "You sound like a politician right now."

Take Charge of Your Life

If you want to be successful (and I know you do), you have to take 100 percent personal responsibility for your life. You will have to give up victim stories or blaming others. Barber's lawsuit blamed others, but it didn't lose him a single pound of fat.

You have to give up any alibis and excuses. Steve Harvey could have had a lot of good excuses, too. He was homeless for three years, divorced twice, lost everything he owned, flunked out of college, and had a stuttering problem.

You have to give up the excuse of being "too old." Colonel Sanders opened his first KFC at age sixty-two. Dave Thomas earned his high school diploma at age sixty-one.

You've got to give up the excuse of always playing it safe because you have a family to support. So did Dave Thomas. As Jim Carrey learned from his father, who decided to forgo his dream of being a comedian to take a safe job as an accountant only to be let go, you can still fail at doing something you hate, so you might as well take a chance on doing what you love.

Here's the good news. If you use the techniques discussed in Chapter 2, you will achieve your goals. It won't happen overnight, *but it will happen.* Those powerful techniques make the alibis and excuses obsolete. The same specific "road-tested" techniques, such as affirmations and visualizations, were used by me, Jim Carrey, and Steve Harvey, and can be harnessed by you to convert your thoughts into reality.

Believe me, I am an ordinary, not extraordinary, person. If I can do it, then you can, too. You don't have to be the Evel Knievel daredevil type. You don't have to be like Steve Harvey and quit your job the next day. All you need, at this juncture, is to align your gifts with your purpose and then take baby-step, educated risks in the direction of your dreams.

TAKEAWAY

Ask yourself, *What if it all goes right?*
Take baby steps that are aligned with your dreams.
The powerful goal-setting formula in Chapter 2
makes alibis and excuses obsolete.

CHAPTER 5
Persistence

*"Persistence is probably the single most common quality of
high achievers. They simply refuse to give up."*
—Jack Canfield

Three of us were running in high-profile races for seats in the
United States House of Representatives back in 2000: me,
future Vice President Mike Pence, and a guy from Illinois. I
won. Pence won. And the Illinois guy lost by thirty-one points. It was
a blowout. I always wondered, *Whatever happened to that guy?* And
then I saw him years later. It was in the checkout line at my local grocery store. He was smiling ear to ear on the cover of *People* magazine.
His name is Barack Obama. He's the guy who "failed" in 2000. I guess
he turned out all right after all, with one Nobel Prize, two terms in
the White House, and three number-one *New York Times* bestsellers.

I served with Barack Obama in Congress for four years (2004–
2008). He is, of course, a gifted speaker and was able to bounce back

nicely after losing his first race for Congress, but his setback was not unique at all. George W. Bush lost his first race for Congress, too. Mike Pence lost his first two races for Congress. Abe Lincoln lost five elections before he captured the White House. In fact, during my lifetime (1964 to the present), 100 percent of the presidents of the United States have lost an election at some point in their career. The point is that *setbacks* happen to everybody. But they're just temporary. So don't quit; *keep going*. The comeback is stronger than the setback.

If you are *aligned* with your purpose and use your gifts, then yes, you will still stumble from time to time and experience temporary setbacks, but you will never fail on any permanent basis.

Jack Canfield: Stories That Inspired the World[36]

Jack Canfield is a master storyteller. As the coauthor of the *Chicken Soup for the Soul* series, he has sold more than 500 million books and holds the Guinness World Record for having seven books on the *New York Times* bestsellers list on the same day—beating out Stephen King.

Jack Canfield's journey provides a remarkable example of the power of persistence. Canfield began his career by teaching at an inner-city high school in Chicago. He noticed right away that his students paid more attention—and were more motivated—when he was telling a story, as opposed to teaching intellectual concepts. Canfield began collecting stories and told his students motivational stories of other young people who grew up in humble circumstances and went on to have successful lives.

Canfield next began training teachers and kept using stories to illustrate his points. Eventually, Canfield shifted into doing seminars and corporate trainings and continued to tell stories. His intuition told him he should put these stories in a book, so he compiled a list of about seventy stories.

He then spoke at a health conference and grabbed lunch with one of the other speakers, Mark Victor Hansen, who would ultimately become the coauthor of the series. Hansen asked Canfield what he was working on, and Canfield told him about the book concept and the seventy stories he had already collected. Hansen wanted to do the project with him and offered a suggestion: "You have to have 101 stories . . . 101 is a spiritual number." They agreed to team up and together collected about 140 stories. They then asked about fifteen people to read all 140 stories and grade them on a scale of one to ten, and the top 101 stories went into the book.

They had a knack for selecting heartwarming stories. For example, one of the selected stories was called "Puppies for Sale." A little boy was walking by a store and saw a sign that said "Puppies for Sale." He went inside and asked, "How much are you charging for the puppies?" The store owner said anywhere from thirty to fifty dollars, depending on the dog. The boy reached into his pocket and out came $2.37. The store owner whistled toward the back and out came eight little puppies.

One of the puppies was limping, and the boy pointed to it and said, "That's the one I want to buy." The store owner said, "You don't want to buy that one; he's got a bad hip socket. He's never gonna be able to run, jump, or play like the other puppies." The boy insisted that he wanted the puppy with a limp and gave the owner his $2.37 and promised to pay fifty cents a month until he paid him off. The owner said, "Yeah, I'll do that. He's never gonna be able to run and jump with you, so why would you want that dog?"

The little boy reached down, and he pulled up his left pant leg. He had a big metal brace on his leg, and he said, "Well, you see, I don't run so well myself, and that little puppy needs someone to understand him, and I need someone to understand me."

Now that they had stories that tugged at the heart, they needed a book title. After meditating for a couple of days, the words "chicken soup" popped into Canfield's head. They wanted to lift people's spirits, so they settled on *Chicken Soup for the Soul*. With the title and compelling stories in hand, Canfield and Hansen met with all the big publishers in New York. None of them wanted the book. The authors were told it would never sell because people don't read collections of short stories. Eventually, Canfield and Hansen went to the annual convention of the American Booksellers Association in Southern California with the *Chicken Soup for the Soul* manuscripts stuffed in their backpacks. They went booth to booth for three days and racked up more rejections. Canfield says that *Chicken Soup for the Soul* was rejected by 144 publishers.

On the final day, Peter Vegso, president of a small South Florida publisher, Health Communications, Inc. (HCI), told them, "I'd like to read the manuscript." Vegso already knew Canfield and had let him and Hansen use the HCI booth as a base of operations. Vegso hadn't looked at the manuscript earlier because, at the time, a collection of stories didn't quite fit into the company's list of mostly recovery books. Peter Vegso told the *Tampa Bay Times*, "I was in the airport reading it, and I was in tears. I had to stop because I thought people would think there was something wrong with a grown man crying in the airport."[37] Vegso's intuition told him this was something special. He had the vision to see what the larger publishers did not and agreed to take the risk and publish the book.

Canfield and Hansen visualized their success and mocked up a *New York Times* bestsellers list showing their book ranked number one. Less than two years later, it happened in real life. The book hit number one on the *New York Times* list and stayed there for three years. The *Chicken Soup for the Soul* book series has been printed in forty-seven languages and has sold more than 500 million copies worldwide. (The tremendous success of these two authors is not accidental. You may wish to briefly revisit the three-step formula in Chapter 2. The bestseller mock-up, the check used by Jim Carrey, or even a photograph are visual aids that give your subconscious a clear picture of what you expect to happen.)

My Rough Start

I grew up in humble circumstances. My mom was a single parent raising three kids. At one point, we all lived together in a rented one-bedroom house with my grandmother. By age thirty-four, I finally had a safe, stable life. I had graduated from Vanderbilt Law School, got married, bought a home, had two kids, and worked at a great law firm.

But I decided to take a risk. At thirty-four, I became an underdog candidate for the U.S. Congress. Because of the lucky breaks I got, my main goal was to increase college financial aid (called Pell Grants) to help kids from low-income families go to college.

The problem was I didn't have any rich friends or political connections. I worked a hundred hours a week nonstop (campaigning, fundraising, and working full-time as a lawyer) but had little to show for it. After about six months, I was behind in the polls by 27 percent, outraised four-to-one, and had zero endorsements. The low point was the day the Florida GOP chairman, Al Cardenas, traveled to Orlando to personally ask me to drop out.

The Hidden Guide

I had reached rock bottom. I felt broken. It seemed as if the whole world wanted me to quit. I knew that if I kept going, the GOP leadership at the local, state, and federal levels would likely be working against me in the primary (and they did). I felt so alone, except for one thing. My intuition was screaming at me, *Keep going. You got this. Everything will be okay. Trust me.* I had no logical reason to trust it, but I did. I didn't hear an audible voice of God, but I might as well have heard it. It was a crystal-clear gut feeling.

I had been tested six ways to Sunday, and this was a do-or-die moment. I told Cardenas, "I'm not quitting. Not now. Not ever. Period." And then, almost magically, things began to turn around. Napoleon Hill wrote about this mysterious phenomenon in *Think and Grow Rich*. He said:

> "There may be no heroic connotation to the word 'persistence,' but the quality is to the character of man what carbon is to steel. . . . Sometimes it appears that there is a hidden Guide whose duty is to test men through all sorts of discouraging experiences. . . . The hidden Guide lets no one enjoy a great achievement without passing the persistence test. . . . What we do not see, what most of us never suspect of existing, is the silent but irresistible power which comes to the rescue of those who fight on in the face of discouragement. If we speak of this power at all we call it persistence, and let it go at that."

Things began to turn around, but in unconventional ways I never expected.

Seinfeld and the Wisdom of George Costanza

After being asked to quit, I went home that night and watched an episode of *Seinfeld* to get my mind off things. In that episode, everything in George's life had been going wrong, so Jerry suggested he do the *opposite*. George agreed and promptly tested his new plan. George noticed a beautiful woman sitting at the diner's counter. Normally, he wouldn't have the courage to approach her, or he would try to act cool. No more. He did the opposite. George walked right up to the pretty lady and said, "My name is George. I am unemployed, and I live with my parents." Amazingly, the new approach worked!

In the final scene, George applied for a job with the New York Yankees. After landing an interview with the Yankees owner George Steinbrenner, George did the opposite one more time:

Steinbrenner: "Nice to meet you."

George: "Well, I wish I could say the same. But I must say, with all due respect, I find it very hard to see the logic behind some of the moves you have made with this fine organization. In the past twenty years, you have caused myself, and the city of New York, a good deal of distress, as we have watched you take our beloved Yankees and reduce them to a laughingstock—all for the glorification of your massive ego!"

Steinbrenner: "Hire this man!"

Ding, ding, ding! That was my sign from the Universe. I should do the opposite. And, to my surprise, it worked for me, too. Things began to turn around.

I changed both my messaging and fundraising strategies. As for my messaging, my stump speech at the time emphasized increasing Pell Grants and promoting mentoring programs. While I was passionate about education topics (and would focus on them in Congress), those were general election issues and not helping me while I was locked in a tough primary battle. So, I switched things up and focused my messaging on cutting taxes and eliminating wasteful spending, which were more primary election issues. I genuinely cared about all four of those topics, but what I was doing wasn't working, so I "did the opposite" and put first things first.

As for fundraising, I sucked at it. And I hated it. I would come up with any excuse not to do it. "Sorry, I've got to rearrange my sock drawer, no time to dial for dollars today." But that wasn't working. So, taking my cues from George Costanza, I did the opposite. I became super persistent, probably too persistent.

I called one guy twenty-one times in a row without success. Twenty-one failures. He was an Amway executive. After twenty-one calls, he finally called me back. He said, "Why do you keep calling me?" I said, "Because I want you to give a thousand dollars to my campaign." He said, "If I give you a thousand dollars, do you promise never to call me again?" I said, "Yes, sir!" He sent the money.

When an Amway sales guy thinks you're too pushy, you know you're too pushy!

The Universe Will Conspire to Help You

"When you want something, all the universe conspires in helping you to achieve it," wrote Paulo Coelho, author of *The Alchemist*.

Twenty years ago, I would have worried that people would think I was some crazy new-age spiritual person if I said that the Universe (God, Life Force) will conspire to help you once you reach a definite decision to burn the ships and risk everything to go after what you want. Now that I am older, I am less concerned about what others may say than I was in the past.

Once the Universe realizes that you refuse to quit and you are willing to stake your life on your mission, it *will* conspire to help you. The Universe will introduce you to people who can help you, plans will pop into your head, and new opportunities will arise. Do not hesitate. Take action immediately. Just like the "Shadow of the Bear" on this book's cover, there will be a narrow window of time to embrace these opportunities. Take advantage of them.

In my case, the Universe "conspired" to help me in a pretty unconventional way: an *American Idol*-style competition, a TV star, and a frog came to the rescue. Really.

The Speech That Changed My World

After Cardenas asked me to quit, I set a goal of raising $400,000 for the primary. I had no idea how I would do it, especially as an underdog in a contested primary. But I wrote down my $400,000 goal on a three-by-five-inch index card. I put it on my nightstand and read it every morning when I woke up and every night before I went to sleep. I also put an extra card in my wallet and looked at it several times throughout the day.

A few weeks later, I got a phone call out of the blue. I was invited to Washington to give a five-minute speech to a newly formed group of CEOs and business executives called the Club for Growth. The Club was considering putting some big money into a handful of congressional races. My new stump speech regarding tax cuts and curbing wasteful spending had caught their attention. They had looked at hundreds of races across the country and narrowed the list down to sixteen finalists.

I flew to Washington on a freezing cold Valentine's Day morning in 2000 as one of the sixteen. Upon arriving, I immediately noticed a couple of familiar faces. Sitting in the Club's audience was former Governor Pete du Pont, a member of the Club who, coincidentally, I had a beer with at Vanderbilt Law School about ten years earlier when he was recruiting for his Delaware law firm. I said hello.

I also noticed Mike Pence and chatted with him backstage. I had met Pence a couple of months earlier on one of my unsuccessful DC PAC fundraising trips. I was happy to see he also made the cut, but this also meant that the competition was fierce. It felt like *American Idol* for politicians.

Wearing my best pinstripe suit and red tie, I stood in the back of the room and listened for hours as the other candidates delivered their smooth pitches. They talked about Laffer curves, marginal income tax rates, capital gains taxes, and supply-side economics.

I needed to stand out, so I opened with that edgy joke about feeling like Elizabeth Taylor's seventh husband on his wedding night and then spoke passionately without notes.

In an article about the speech, "Talk to Big-Money Donors Changed Keller's Life," the *Orlando Sentinel* wrote about the group's assessment of me: "Keller scored 11s on a scale of 1 to 10." The group ranked me number one in the country and spent $400,000 to support me. It was, coincidentally, the exact amount of my goal. Money would no longer be an object, and I could, at least, continue until the primary election day.

Morning Joe Gives Me a Boost

I came in a distant second on the GOP primary election night. The GOP frontrunner, a state representative, got 43 percent, and I only got 31 percent of the vote. It felt like a punch in the stomach. At the time, Florida election law required a candidate to get at least 50 percent of the vote. Since neither of the top two candidates technically got 50 percent, it threw the race into a runoff election to be held a month away. Still, because I was so far behind, everyone thought the race was over and asked me to quit.

Florida GOP Chairman Al Cardenas personally visited my office again and asked me to quit—the second such request. One of my key staffers asked me to quit "for the good of the party" and then resigned when I refused to give up. Donors asked for their money back. A local newspaper took notice and wrote, "Keller's own Republican Party abandoned him." It was a dark moment.

What did I do? I didn't quit. I went all in. I risked *everything* I owned. I spent every penny of my savings account. I maxed out both my credit cards. I even took out a home equity loan. I wore out the soles of my shoes by walking door to door through the neighborhoods I had lost in order to personally meet the voters.

Did I know something the pessimists didn't? Sort of, yes. First, I had learned from the prior incident (when they asked me to quit) that when you take risks to move toward your purpose, the Universe (God, Infinite Intelligence) will conspire to help you.

Second, I had faith that it was "possible" to fail and win anyway. For example, I knew that Joe Scarborough, then a congressman from North Florida, also came in second in his first GOP primary election with the identical 31 percent of the vote, but he still went on to win. I wondered if Scarborough would help me, but I knew it was unlikely. The overwhelming majority of sitting members of Congress will not interject themselves into a hotly contested primary battle because they will have to work with the eventual winner, and they don't know who that will be.

But I asked him anyway, and he said yes. It is almost as if angels are waiting to help you once they see you are willing to risk it all on a single turn of the wheel. During the runoff, Scarborough inspired me, endorsed me, donated to me, did three campaign events for me, loaned me his political director (Derek Kitts) for a month, and mentored me. The result: we did what the haters said couldn't be done. We went from 31 percent to 52 percent and won the GOP nomination. Scarborough is now the host of *Morning Joe* on MSNBC.

The Frog That Went Viral

After becoming the GOP nominee, I had lots of new best friends. The biggest stars in politics lined up to help me during the final two weeks of the campaign, including no less than four GOP nominees for president: Bob Dole, George Bush, George W. Bush, and John McCain. Presidents and senators dropped what they were doing and came to Orlando to help me. Did it make a difference? Was I too much of an underdog?

How in the world could I win the general election against a popular mayor who had once been ahead of me in the polls by a jaw-dropping 27 percentage points? Ironically, the Universe sent a frog to help me hop over the finish line. When my general election opponent was mayor, she spent $18,500 in taxpayer money on a bronze frog sculpture. The frog, about three feet tall, sat next to a pond in a public park in west Orange County. The frog became a symbol of wasteful spending.

The frog controversy went viral. The frog had become more famous than Kermit. It was on the nightly TV news and in newspapers across the country, including the *New York Times* and *Washington Post*. With control of Congress hanging in the balance, even the most powerful congressional leaders joined the frog battle. For example, the second-most powerful man in the U.S. House of Representatives, Majority Leader Dick Armey, flew down to Orlando and held a press conference standing next to the bronze frog, saying in essence, "We've got to do something about these damn frogs and wasteful spending." And that was just the "free" media.

As for "paid" media, over a million dollars was spent on television ads, radio ads, and campaign mailers by outside groups and political parties for and against the frog. Literally, a million-dollar dispute over an $18,500 frog.

"The frog now sits on political center stage, featured in both Republican and Democratic television ads and copied onto thousands of campaign mailers," wrote the *Orlando Sentinel*.[38]

A voter walked up to me on the sidewalks of downtown Orlando, gave me a high-five, and said, "I love that frog thing, man." For thirty crazy days, the frog had become the main conversation topic at the water coolers at work, in Central Florida coffee shops, and on talk radio.

Why so much attention to a silly frog? On the one hand, those people who were "against" the bronze frog thought it was a waste of taxpayer dollars. To them, the frog was tangible, relatable, and represented a whole year's salary for some folks.

On the other hand, people who were "for" the frog were hopping mad at me—calling me "frog-o-phobic," "amphibian-obsessed," and a few unprintable names—because they were passionate supporters of public funding for the arts.

By election night, the light-hearted issue had leap-frogged me from 27 percent behind in the polls to a dead-even fifty-fifty tie.

The infamous bronze frog statue that helped swing my election.

Chilling in the Hotel Bathroom

It was election night, about 10 PM on Tuesday, November 7, 2000. The polls had been closed for hours, and the race was tied at 50 percent each. "It's too close to call," the TV anchorman said. "Looks like the vote counting between George W. Bush and Al Gore will take a while. But stay tuned. We should be able to call the race for Congress shortly after the remaining absentee ballots are counted." As the TV reporter spoke, a banner slowly scrolled across the bottom of the TV screen that told the story: "U.S. Congress, District 8, Keller 50% Chapin 50%, Keller up 600 votes, 10,000 absentee votes yet to be counted."

I was the underdog. With 10,000 absentee ballot votes still left to count, my tiny 600-vote lead could be gone in a New York minute. Maybe it already was. After all, about 92 percent of the remaining absentee ballots were from Orange County, where my opponent had been a popular mayor. On the other hand, we had a great absentee ballot program, too; every person who requested an absentee ballot immediately got a glossy campaign mailer from us.

I felt so out of control. I needed to be alone. My life would turn on what happened in the next few minutes. "Jason, I can't watch it. I'm just going to chill in the bathroom," I told my campaign manager Jason Miller. "Sure, man. I'll let you know," he replied.

I entered the bathroom, shut the door, cut the lights off, and took a seat in the darkness. On a scale of one to ten, the tension level I felt was an eleven. As I waited for the outcome, I replayed the last year and a half of my life over and over in my mind. It was a highlight reel of the campaign's emotional turning points.

I thought about the start of my campaign. Nobody gave me a chance. I didn't know how I would do my day job as a lawyer and run for Congress at the same time. Big law firms (like the one where

I worked) had significant billable-hour requirements, and I was up for partner that year, which meant added pressure to work long hours. I managed to do both jobs and make partner, too, but the workload nearly killed me. As I sat alone in the dark, I kept wondering, *Was all this for nothing?*

I thought about how unconventional my campaign had been. Are other races decided by frogs, *Seinfeld* episodes, and *American Idol*-like competitions? The one common denominator along the crazy and chaotic path leading to election night is that I trusted my instincts no matter how unconventional or unpopular they seemed.

Although there were some small victories along the eighteen-month journey, there were just as many low points and setbacks. I relived them, too. I saw that pit bull in the front yard as I walked door to door to meet voters. It scared the hell out of me, but I made myself walk up to the door anyway. I told myself, *Suck it up. This could be the vote that decides it.*

I remembered sitting on the couch one evening, watching the local news. They aired three anti-Keller TV attack ads in a row from outside groups. I remembered thinking, *Hmmm, maybe I do suck. Was it all for nothing?*

I thought about all those dreadful fundraising calls. I hated them, but I told myself, *No money, no TV ads,* and forced myself to do it.

I thought back to the GOP primary election night when I came in second. It felt like a punch in the stomach.

As I replayed the campaign's highs and lows in my mind, I was jolted back to reality by three loud knocks on the bathroom door.

I knew that meant a decision had been made, but I had no idea what it was. I closed my eyes and took a deep breath to steel myself for the decision.

My campaign manager flung open the door, flicked on the lights, and delivered the news:

"You *won*, my man!" The newspaper headline said it all: "Mr. Keller Goes to Washington."[39]

"Aunt" Helen Keller

I've always loved this quote from Helen Keller: "We can do anything we want to do if we stick to it long enough." Ever since I was a little kid, as soon as people find out my name is Ric Keller, the first thing most people ask is, "Are you related to Helen Keller?" I am pretty sure that I am not. I'm not a "natural-born" Keller. I was born Ric Orenstein. It was only after my mom remarried when I was four years old that I was given my stepfather's last name of Keller.

Still, I am proud to share her last name. I always secretly want to lie and say, "Yes, we are related!" And why not? She was the first blind and deaf person to graduate from college in the United States (Harvard, no less), and Winston Churchill called her "the greatest woman of our age." And she made *Time*'s list of the 100 most influential people of the twentieth century, right up there with Albert Einstein and Mahatma Gandhi.

I even rationalize to myself why the lie might be justified. I don't "technically" have Helen Keller's DNA, but I do share some of the same Keller traits. She was optimistic, she took chances, she was persistent, and she loved to joke around. And yet, each time I'm asked about my most famous "relative," I just tell the truth. When I'm asked if I'm related, I just reply, "I wish I was related. Helen Keller was blind and deaf and still graduated from Harvard. I can see and hear and still got fired from Wendy's."

"Aunt" Helen was funny. She was friends with Mark Twain, who loved her sense of humor and sharp intellect. Twain even convinced one of his wealthy friends to pay for Keller's Harvard education. She had a fun-loving human side. She loved to drink her martinis, and during Prohibition, toured the country with Anne Sullivan for five years as part of a vaudeville act. During her show, Keller held Q&A sessions with the audience and showcased her humor. For example, when an audience member asked, "What do you think is the most important question before the country today?" she replied, "How to get a drink." When another audience member asked, "Can you see any way out of our troubles?" Keller replied, "Have you thought of divorce?"[40]

Helen Keller's whole life is a testament to the power of persistence. When she was only nineteen months old, she contracted a fever that would leave her deaf and blind. With the help of her beloved teacher, Anne Sullivan, Keller learned to read and write. After graduating from Harvard, she wrote fourteen books and traveled the world as an advocate for the blind. Her autobiography was turned into a Broadway play and Hollywood movie. The play won the Tony Award, and the movie won an Academy Award. Helen Keller even won an Oscar herself at age seventy-five when a documentary based on her life won the Academy Award for Best Documentary.

Sweating with Richard Simmons

I've struggled with weight my whole life.

It didn't start out so bad. As a kid, playing sports and staying active kept my weight in check. I played football from first grade through my senior year of high school and typically played outside after school.

But after high school, it was a frustrating yo-yo for decades—mainly because of a stagnant lifestyle and emotional eating. My kryptonite was Little Debbie Oatmeal Creme Pies. By my early forties, I was in my fourth term in Congress, and my weight had ballooned up to 255 pounds. It was sad because I used to be a pretty good athlete.

The rock-bottom moment was in June 2007. I was talking with one of my colleagues on the House floor during votes. He mentioned that someone said to one of his staff members, "Has anyone ever told you that you look a lot like Ric Keller?" The staffer replied, "Ric Keller? I better hit the gym!" I laughed at the story, but it secretly hurt my feelings. I felt like a joke.

It was a turning point. I decided to quietly make some changes. The next morning, I called an Orlando nutritionist named Tara Gidus, the team dietitian for the Orlando Magic NBA team. I remember our first appointment.

Me: "I know I have to eat better, but I hate vegetables like spinach, broccoli, and cauliflower."

Tara: "Then don't eat them. Which ones do you like?"

Me: "Salads, green beans, cucumbers, and tomatoes. That's about it."

Tara: "Then eat that. You've got to live with it."

She put me on an 1,800-calorie diet designed to help me lose about two pounds a week. I also got a journal, and for the first time, logged my daily exercise and calories.

My exercise program had a modest beginning. It was baby steps. On my first day of exercising, I jogged for only five minutes. It was the same for each day that week. The second week, I bumped up slightly to ten minutes each day. Baby steps. I added only five minutes a week. After three months, I was running an hour every morning.

After four to five months, my colleagues on both sides of the aisle started to comment on the positive changes in my appearance. Even

Rep. Rahm Emanuel (D-IL), who chaired the Democratic Congressional Campaign Committee (DCCC) and would later become the mayor of Chicago, encouraged me to stay on track. For example, I always carried around an insulated lunch box with a couple of apples in it as healthy snacks. One day I forgot it. Emanuel noticed and remarked, "Keller, where're the apples? Get your shit together!"

Weight struggles are bipartisan, even with well-respected high achievers. Ask Oprah Winfrey and Chris Christie. My own weight struggles made me a better, more bipartisan congressman. We have far more things in common than we have differences. I joined the bipartisan House Fitness Caucus, founded by Zach Wamp (R-TN) and co-chaired by Ron Kind (D-WI), a former Harvard quarterback. The Fitness Caucus promoted PE in schools and sought bipartisan solutions to obesity-related problems.

My weight continued to come off at about two pounds a week. After one year, I stepped on the scale. I had lost a hundred pounds. Congressman Wamp held a press conference with Richard Simmons and named me the "Fitness Caucus Hero of the Decade."

There was an unexpected perk from working out in the House gym. I got advice from world-class athletes. For example, Rep. Jim Ryun (R-KS), an Olympic medalist in running, showed me how to stretch after my runs. It kept me injury-free. Also, Rep. Jim Jordan (R-OH), who was the two-time NCAA wrestling national champion, taught me about using interval training on the treadmill. The interval training lessons made me more efficient with my time—and helped me successfully break through frustrating weight-loss plateaus.

Having seen these healthy habits transform my life, I wanted to pay it forward somehow and help others. I co-sponsored the bipartisan Fit Kids Act legislation to bring physical education back into public schools. Also, I orchestrated a congressional hearing by the House Education Committee on "The Benefits of Physical Education for Our Nation's Children," which was how I met Richard Simmons.

The witnesses included Congressmen Zach Wamp and Ron Kind (who coauthored the Fit Kids Act), 1987 Heisman Trophy winner and 2015 Pro Football Hall of Fame inductee Tim Brown, and Richard Simmons, the well-known fitness advocate with an energetic personality.

Since I served on the Education Committee, I took the lead at the hearing by giving an opening statement and questioning the witnesses. I had seen Richard Simmons many times before on David Letterman and heard him on Howard Stern's radio show. Most people knew Simmons from his aerobic dance videos called "Sweatin' to the Oldies."

Richard Simmons arrived at the hearing dressed up in a suit and tie. He gave a passionate speech. Among other things, Simmons said:

"I was not a jock. I spent my elementary school, my high school, and my college sitting on the benches watching everyone play sports. And to get back at them, while they were playing sports, I ate their lunch. I was 268 pounds.

"I was twenty-three years old when I took my first exercise class. I was bitten by the sweat bug. I am not 268 pounds anymore. And I am still not a jock. But I am fit.

"I do not want any child in America to have my childhood because it was taken away from me because I just wasn't good enough. Well, I am good enough now. And I have devoted my life to this, and I will devote my life to this to the day I die. And I hope that one day every kid gets to feel the self-esteem and self-respect that I have."

Wow! I was truly impressed. The message, the delivery, and the authenticity: Simmons was made for this moment. During my eight years in Congress, I saw some remarkable speeches by presidents, foreign heads of state, fellow members of Congress, ambassadors, and celebrities. Richard Simmons's speech at our congressional hearing was the single best speech I've ever heard.

I asked Simmons a few follow-up questions and casually mentioned that my own journey taught me that exercise can also be a great stress-reducer.

Me: "By exercising, I'm not stressed anymore."

Simmons: "And you're cute!"

Me (laughing): "Okay, now I'm stressed."

The audience in the hearing room at the Rayburn House Office Building spontaneously erupted in laughter. The funny exchange was televised on C-SPAN and written about by the *Washington Post* and *The Hill* newspapers.

Questioning fitness advocate Richard Simmons at a 2008 House Education Committee hearing.

After the official hearing concluded, Simmons changed into his trademark candy-striped shorts and a bedazzled red tank top. He then joined Zach Wamp, Ron Kind, and me for an outdoor press conference on Capitol Hill. A huge crowd had gathered to see the celebrity fitness trainer in person.

I had the honor of introducing Richard Simmons. After I handed him the microphone, Simmons did what he did best. He gave an upbeat talk and then put on some dance music. Within minutes, he had everybody "Sweatin' to the Oldies." After the press conference, Richard Simmons invited me to be his guest on the Sirius XM radio show called *Lighten Up with Richard Simmons,* and I was happy to do it.

I haven't seen Richard Simmons since that time, but I'll always remember the day he took over Capitol Hill. One way or the other, Simmons got us all sweating that day—some through dancing, and me from a "you're cute" compliment.

Getting Help

Although I was successful in losing weight, *maintaining* the weight loss was still a struggle. I had to do about an hour of cardio a day. I was constantly hungry. And I felt at war with my body.

I read an article about a surgeon from Vanderbilt Medical School who discussed the positive benefits of a relatively new procedure called sleeve gastrectomy (commonly referred to as "the sleeve"). After looking into it further, I learned that it was a minimally invasive surgical procedure that simply reduced the size of your stomach without changing any of the other normal digestive anatomy or processes. By changing the shape of your stomach, it makes you feel full much faster and reduces emotional eating.

The studies I read showed that the sleeve procedure had excellent success rates ranging from 80 percent to 90 percent, the majority of people kept most of the weight off for the long term, and it improved health, as evidenced by the fact that diabetes went into remission and blood pressure numbers improved in three out of four patients.

I decided to give it a try. It was one of the most positive things I've ever done. It improved my health and self-image. After the procedure, I was confident about keeping the weight off, so I exercised like crazy with weights and cardio training to get in the best shape of my life. But there was still a problem. The permanent weight loss had left excess sagging skin on my waist that wouldn't go away no matter how many sit-ups I did or miles I jogged. It was disheartening. I decided to do something about it by having an abdominoplasty (aka, tummy tuck) to have the excess skin removed. I loved the result and felt better about myself.

Many years ago, I wouldn't have had the courage to be vulnerable about this type of thing. I would have worried that people might judge me and think I was "weak" or somehow cheating by getting procedures that helped me control my hunger and remove the sagging skin. But I know I'm not weak, and I worked darn hard to lose the weight, and there was nothing I could do to fix the sagging skin. Now that I'm older, I'm not as concerned with what others may think. Rather, my only wish is to help others. I am sharing this personal story to offer some hope to you and others who may face similar struggles.

Here's the *Reader's Digest* version: Regardless of whether your goal is losing weight, earning money, getting straight A's, or something else, be persistent, take baby steps, and work hard. But if you ever need help—whether it is dealing with depression, maintaining weight loss, or removing excess skin—don't be ashamed at all about getting the help you need.

I'm not a doctor and don't play one on TV, so I'm not writing this section to give any medical advice. You and your doctor should decide what is best for you. But what I am saying is that if you feel that someone can help you—whether it be a nutritionist, personal trainer, psychologist, peer group, tutor, or doctor—don't feel any shame whatsoever in taking positive steps to do what is best for your physical and mental health. Life isn't practice, and 99 percent of the people will be rooting for you to succeed.

TAKEAWAY

Don't give up. Once the Universe realizes that you refuse to quit, it will conspire to help you. If you are aligned with your purpose and use your gifts, you may stumble but you will never fail on a permanent basis.

CHAPTER 6
Fail, Pivot, and Win

"It is impossible to live without failing at something, unless you live so cautiously that you might as well not have lived at all. In which case, you fail by default."
— J. K. Rowling

You can fail and win anyway. If your first plan fails, try a new one. If that plan fails, try another. Just keep moving in the direction of your goal. When most people meet with failure, they quit instead of creating new plans to replace those that failed.

Making Halftime Adjustments to Win the Game

Every great football coach knows that halftime adjustments are needed when the original game plan is not working out. Tom Osborne, the legendary Nebraska Cornhuskers head football coach, was elected to Congress at the same time as me. We sat next to each other on the House Education Committee for six years.

As the winner of three national championships, Coach Osborne was known for making great halftime adjustments. For example, in 1983, Nebraska led Iowa State 14–12 at halftime. After making significant halftime adjustments, Nebraska quickly pulled ahead. The score was 62–19 by the end of the third quarter. It set an NCAA record for "most points scored in a brief period of time" by putting up forty-eight points in only nine minutes.

We need the same approach in life off the football field. For example, Pam Grout wrote a book called *God Doesn't Have Bad Hair Days*. It was a clever book that included several do-it-yourself experiments to prove "thoughts are things" that emit energy, but the book flopped. Grout believed in the book, and she came up with a new plan. About seven years later, she repurposed the book, got a new publisher, got a new book cover, and renamed it *E-Squared*. Subsequently, *E-Squared* became a number-one *New York Times* bestseller.

Pam Grout essentially made some "halftime adjustments" that made all the difference.

When I ran for Congress as an underdog in 2000, my campaign team made some key halftime adjustments that turned things around. The GOP favorite got 43 percent in the primary, and I came in a distant second with 31 percent.

I didn't know why I had done so poorly. My campaign manager, Jason Miller, analyzed the detailed votes by precinct and saw the problem. My opponent, a state representative, was able to rack up 43 percent of the vote in the primary, in part, by crushing us in the precincts within his old state house seat.

Miller gave me a list of specific precincts within my opponent's old state house seat that had voted for the more conservative candidate in a state house race on the same day. I noticed they were the more blue-collar GOP areas, with regular folks like me who ate at Cracker Barrel and shopped at Bass Pro Shops. Since I was the underdog outsider, those should be my people. Within each of those targeted precincts, my team gave me a list of so-called Super Voters who always show up in primaries.

We figured that this list of Super Voters in these targeted districts would possibly switch their votes and vote for me. But it required the personal touch—and a lot of legwork. Taylor Ford, an eighteen-year-old enthusiastic campaign aide, was assigned to walk these targeted neighborhoods with me every night for a month.

On one occasion, as he stood next to a voter, I heard him from across the street: "There he is! Across the street! Your next congress-man! Ric Keller! Wanna meet him?" I walked over and shook the voter's hand. We had been on TV a lot, and the voter looked surprised to see me at his home. Our conversation was typical of many others:

Voter: "What are you doing here?"

Me: "I'm Ric Keller. I'm running for Congress. I'd love your vote in the runoff."

Voter: "I know who you are. But I'm a Sublette guy. He's been my state rep for years."

Me: "He's a good guy. I can see why you support him. But can I ask you one question?"

Voter: "Sure."

Me: "Did he ever personally come to your home?"

Voter: "No."

Me: "Well, I'm here. And I'll be here if you ever need me. You can count on me—can I count on you?"

We won him over . . . and many others, too. "Eighty percent of success is showing up," Woody Allen said.

We flipped precinct after precinct. On October 3, 2000, we won the runoff 52 percent to 48 percent.

We were able to fail, pivot, and win anyway; just like Pam Grout and Tom Osborne. You can, too. None of us is perfect, but a little humility and persistence can go a long way. Be willing to make half-time adjustments.

Making the Most of a Universe-Sized Mix-up

Steve Harvey was on top of the world. A shelf full of Emmy Awards, host of two hit TV shows, a number-one *New York Times* bestselling book, a hit movie, a nationally syndicated radio show, one of the Original Kings of Comedy, married to the love of his life, and a reported net worth of $200 million.

What could go wrong? On December 21, 2015, Harvey hosted the Miss Universe pageant and mistakenly crowned first runner-up Miss Colombia as the winner.[41] The real winner was Miss Philippines. He read the wrong name. The crown was literally removed from Miss Colombia's head and placed on Miss Philippines. It was one of the most high-profile, embarrassing moments in the history of television.

The next day, Steve Harvey's name was Googled two billion times and appeared on the front page of newspapers in sixty-four countries.[42] There was plenty of blame to go around, but Harvey accepted responsibility and made the decision to walk back onstage and fix things immediately. In a graduation speech to Alabama State University, Harvey said, "I shamed myself. It was humiliating. It was a week of agonizing humiliation." He received death threats that forced him to hire security guards.[43]

However, he made it through the storm and showed how it was possible to fail and win anyway. First, T-Mobile paid him millions of dollars to film a Super Bowl commercial that was a riff on the accident. "They paid me so much money I'd go out and say the wrong name next year again," Harvey joked. Second, the *Steve Harvey* talk show received its highest TV ratings ever when Miss Colombia subsequently appeared on his show.[44] She graciously forgave him and joked, "Well, at least I still got to be Miss Universe for four and a half minutes." And third, Harvey had the courage to use self-deprecating humor on Christmas morning 2015 (four days after the pageant), when he authorized his team to post a photograph of himself holding a cigar with the caption, "Merry Easter, y'all."[45]

People don't expect you to be perfect; they expect you to be human and kind when possible. By the way, it's always possible. Steve Harvey is a great example of how—with courage, humor, and a positive attitude—you can fail and win anyway.

John Boehner's Comeback

I first met John Boehner ten years before he was elected Speaker of the U.S. House of Representatives. At the time, Boehner was the newly appointed chairman of the House Education Committee, and I was a freshman assigned to his committee. He was affable, perpetually tanned, and loved to relax with merlot wine, Camel cigarettes, and tee times.

This little behind-the-scenes story is a good example of how you can fail, pivot, and win anyway. John Boehner was elected to Congress in 1990 (R-OH). In 1994, he was elected chairman of the House Republican Conference (the fourth most powerful Republican in the GOP leadership).

When the GOP lost seats in the 1998 elections, several members of the Republican leadership team faced internal challengers. Boehner lost his chairmanship to former Oklahoma quarterback J.C. Watts. Boehner was the only one who lost, and it was a tough blow for him.

When I arrived in DC after the November 2000 elections, Boehner had just been named chairman of the House Education Committee. President George W. Bush had campaigned on education reform as one of his top three issues. This gave Boehner a high-profile role in shepherding the president's controversial reform bill, called No Child Left Behind, through Congress.

I had my first sit-down meeting with Boehner in January 2001. He asked to meet with me to learn my top three priorities for his committee.

Boehner: "I got eleven brothers and sisters, and my dad owned a bar, so I can spot bullshit a mile away. Tell me what you really want, and I'll let you know where I can help."

Me: "Thanks for asking, Mr. Chairman. I want to help poor kids go to college by increasing Pell Grants."

Boehner: "I think that's a great idea, and I'm going to help you."

Me: "Second, I'd love to see more grants promote mentoring programs."

Boehner: "I don't know about that one. Let's see."

Me: "Third, I'd like to see more school construction funding to help get kids out of portable trailers and into classrooms."

Boehner: "It'll never happen. Not enough money in the entire federal budget. Local issue anyway." (He was right.)

To his credit, Boehner did exactly what he said he would do.

There were lots of good leaders in Washington, but there were three things about Boehner that were unique. First, he was a straight shooter in terms of how he talked and acted. He told you bluntly exactly what he thought, and he did what he said he would do. He helped me become chairman of the Higher Education Subcommittee and to increase Pell Grant funding. During my time in Congress, Pell Grant funding went up 62 percent, five million poor kids went to college, and several of my Pell Grant bills became law. Because of my focus on Pell Grants, Boehner nicknamed me "Mr. Peller."

Second, he insisted on civility and was great at keeping the temperature down. For example, members of the committee were free to vigorously disagree (and argue) with each other's positions, but it was considered out of order to question their motives. In other words, it's fine to say, "That amendment is bad policy and will cause thousands of people to lose their jobs." It's not okay to say, "You are only offering that amendment because the unions gave you $100,000 in campaign contributions." Not civil and not appropriate to question the sincerity of another member's motivation.

Third, he was empathetic to our concerns. For example, the committee members got to ask questions in the order of their seniority. As a freshman, I spent a lot of time preparing for the hearings but never got to ask questions. The hearings were optional. So, in the private room before the next public hearing took place, I said to Boehner, "Screw this. This is my last hearing. I'm tired of busting my ass to get ready and then not being able to ask questions." When the hearing started that morning, Boehner said, "We're going to do things differently today. The first person to ask questions today will be Mr. Keller of Florida." It was classy. He didn't have to do that. I never complained about anything again.

His combination of those skills made me think he'd be a good leader for the whole House. Boehner's exile from the GOP leadership had lasted seven years.

His shot for a comeback to GOP leadership happened when Tom DeLay stepped down as Majority Leader. The vote to replace DeLay was scheduled for February 2006. The stakes were high because the winner would likely be the future Speaker of the House.

John Boehner threw his hat in the ring. It was an unconventional route to power for three reasons. First, he had lost a lower-rung leadership position. Second, he chaired a less-desirable "B" committee (Education). (The more powerful positions were typically chairmen of the "A" committees, such as Appropriations or Ways and Means, which controlled money and taxes.) Third, he was trying to win the top spot over the Establishment favorite and current Majority Whip, Roy Blunt, who was the heavy favorite to win. It would be a traditional move to bump up one slot from Whip to Majority Leader. Since there were 232 Republicans, it took 117 votes (50 percent plus one) to win, and the *New York Times* reported that Roy Blunt had already collected enough vote pledges to seal the deal.

Another lawmaker, Rep. John Shadegg (R-AZ), who had a conservative following, also joined the race. Boehner and Shadegg were considered underdogs.

I was the only Florida congressman supporting Boehner. The Florida GOP congressional delegation held a conference call in the days leading up to the vote to discuss the matter. Rep. Clay Shaw, the dean of the Florida delegation, kicked off the conversation: "We should announce that the entire Florida delegation is unanimously supporting Roy Blunt. He's going to win anyway, and we'll get credit for putting him over the top."

Since Blunt was only a handful of votes away from collecting enough public pledges to win the race outright, the others on the call agreed. Except me. "Guys, I'm supporting Boehner. He's my chairman on the Education Committee. I've never seen anybody better at keeping the temperature down when members disagree. He will be a great Majority Leader," I said.

I was the only Florida member on the Education Committee. Therefore, having worked closely with Boehner for five years, I knew him much better than the others did.

My refusal to go along with the group ticked off at least two of my Florida peers, and they said so. It was a contentious call. They had lots of seniority and hoped to become chairmen of two important committees. They were Blunt supporters and thought he was the ticket to their chairmen's gavels. They thought I was screwing things up for them, especially since Blunt's victory was a foregone conclusion.

Still, I wasn't budging. And I said so. "Listen guys, I love Roy Blunt for a lot of reasons. And I think he'd be a great leader, too. He's worthy of supporting. But I'm voting for Boehner. It's not up for debate."

It was not pleasant. Toward the end of the call, Rep. Adam Putnam, who was a Blunt supporter, piped up and suggested that the others lay off. Although Putnam was the youngest member of Congress, he was wise beyond his years: "What if Ric is right? If Boehner wins, it might be a good thing for Florida to have somebody on the inside with a Boehner connection."

The call ended. I was alone. Ralph Waldo Emerson once said: "It is easy in the world to live after the world's opinion; it is easy in solitude to live after our own, but the great man is he who in the midst of the crowd keeps with perfect sweetness the independence of solitude."

I don't hold myself out as a "great man." But I do follow my instincts—no matter how unpopular or unconventional they may seem. My instincts, despite all logic to the contrary, told me that Boehner should win and would win.

On February 3, 2006, the secret ballot vote took place inside a large, closed-door conference room. It took 117 votes to win. Blunt received 110 votes, Boehner 79, and Shadegg 40. Jim Ryun, a former Olympic medalist, wasn't on the ballot but still got two votes.

Roy Blunt was way far ahead (as predicted), but since Blunt came up just seven votes shy of the 117-vote majority he needed to win, the race was forced into a second round of voting. Shadegg then quickly endorsed Boehner and urged his supporters to do the same. Boehner had also lobbied others, including a couple of my Florida colleagues, to consider supporting him in the second round, even if they voted for someone else the first time.

The leadership staff passed out the ballots for a second round and then collected the slips of paper. It was high drama as we awaited the announcement.

The tally was announced: "John Boehner 122 votes. Roy Blunt 109 votes."

It was a shocker. The dark horse candidate was the new GOP Majority Leader and future Speaker of the House of Representatives. It was one of the most unconventional and surprising comebacks in political history.

After he won, we all waited in this closed-door meeting for Boehner to address us for the first time as our official new leader. He walked to the front of the room and began to speak. It was emotional. He choked up talking about the pain of being tossed out of leadership in 1998, and the long road back. For seven years in exile, he kept his nose to the grindstone and helped raise money for other members. As he reflected on the tough climb back, he began to cry again. To paraphrase singer Lesley Gore, it was his party, and he could cry if wanted to.

I loved it all—the persistence, the outcome, the touching speech, and the lesson. You can fail and win anyway. Boehner's comeback reminds me of an old story. A man goes out to get the paper from the front steps, and he sees a snail. The man picks up the snail and throws it across the yard. Three years later, there is a knock at the door. The man answers the door and sees the snail. The snail says, "What did you do that for?" (I think I heard the story from Drew Carey.)

There was one other perk. Shortly after Boehner's victory, I was promoted to chairman of the Higher Education Subcommittee and received my own gavel. (I used my new gavel to conk those two senior congressmen over the head. Just kidding.) My new role helped me to achieve my goals of expanding Pell Grants, which helped five million students from low-income families go to college.

Let Failure Fuel Your Success

Michael Jordan turned failure into a positive by using it to fuel his preparation, training, and success. Jordan said, "Twenty-six times I've been trusted to take the game-winning shot and missed. I've failed over and over again in my life. And that is why I succeed."

Other great athletes do as well. Abby Wambach is the Michael Jordan of soccer. She scored more professional goals than anyone else in soccer history, along with winning World Cup championships and Olympic gold medals. While she has demonstrated amazing talent since she began playing at age five, she was self-admittedly rebellious, not always 100 percent committed to her health and training, and experienced defeat many times. Yet she believes failure fuels success, not just for her but for everyone.

As a player on the Youth National Team, Wambach visited the locker room of the US Women's National Team. Her most vivid memory was a five-by-seven photograph of the Norwegian national team celebrating their World Cup victory over the USA taped next to the door leading to the training field. She didn't understand why the team would want to be reminded of their defeat.

Five years later, when she was a rookie on the National Team, she was able to ask her teammates why that picture was on the locker room wall. The veteran players gladly explained that there are many lessons that can be learned from failure, which can become "the fuel for tomorrow's win." And it had worked because the next year, they won their first Olympic gold medal.

Wambach realized that to be a champion, she'd need to spend her life "transforming [her] failures into successes," which she actually had already been doing.

She experienced a devastating loss in the high school state championship game her senior year, which propelled her to "try harder and never give up."[47]

When Wambach was part of the University of Florida Gators women's soccer team, their only loss one season was to the dominant North Carolina Tar Heels. This devastating loss in an otherwise undefeated season inspired the team's later victory against that same team in the NCAA Championship.

The pain of a World Cup loss to Germany in 2003—and resulting self-reflection and analysis—fueled a difficult, gold medal-winning Olympic victory against Brazil in 2004. A horrific leg injury that caused her to miss the Beijing Olympics in 2008 inspired a comeback, the scoring of her one hundredth goal a year later, and another gold medal in 2012.

According to Wambach, "It's not your failures that define you, but how you react to them and use them to change. You should all ask yourself three questions: Where do you want to go? How do you want to get there? And why?"[48]

My Dance with Failures

I don't approach this topic of failure from a high and mighty perspective. I've danced with failure more than a few times but lived to tell about it. I've been fat and thin, poor and rich, divorced and married, depressed and happy, unknown and well-known (in Orlando), victorious and defeated. I'll candidly talk about my most painful failure.

I was blessed to be able to serve four terms in Congress. In 2008, Barack Obama, who had lost a race for the U.S. House in 2000 (the year I won), ran for president. The country had soured on the Iraq War. It was a tidal-wave election. The Democrats captured the White House, the Senate, and the House. The GOP members of Congress in swing seats across the country, including me, were all tossed out of office.

While I ran ahead of McCain—who was popular with independents—and the other GOP congressmen, it wasn't enough to overcome the dramatic spike in Democratic voter turnout because of the Obama factor (he carried my state, county, city, and congressional district). I narrowly lost 48 percent to 52 percent.

My eight-year tour of duty was over. Logically, I knew that I had done a good job and that wave elections aren't personal. I knew firsthand that other really good congressmen also lost their seats in wave elections.

Still, the truth is that the loss was very painful. I took it personally. I felt rejected. The morning after the election, I pulled into a gas station to fill up my car. My credit card was declined. I thought, *Shit, I can't win.*

I had never been to a counselor or taken an antidepressant medication in my life, but I did (Wellbutrin) after this loss. In terms of sadness, on a scale of one to ten, it was a ten. I hope you won't feel any shame at all if you are ever depressed or anxious and need to talk to someone. I was so down that, in my darkest moment, I put pen to paper and wrote a country song about how I was feeling! How cliché, right? The first verse was:

"I fell from the sky, after flying so high, I know how rock bottom feels.

The fame's all gone, the crowds have moved on And I'm numbing the pain with some pills."

But Napoleon Hill was right: "Every adversity carries with it the seed of an equivalent benefit." In my case, there were three major benefits: humility, more money, and more quality time with my kids.

I'll start with the humility part. I went back to practicing law in Orlando. My first case was a small one. An insurance company hired me to defend a business whose truck driver was at fault for causing a minor rear-end collision. The first thing I did was telephone the owner of the company to introduce myself. I said, "Hi, I'm Ric Keller. I'm going to be handling the defense of this lawsuit for you."

He said, "Ric Keller, huh? There is also a congressman named Ric Keller. Have you ever heard of him?"

"Yes."

"Do you know him?"

"Yes."

"Are you him?"

"Yes."

"Oh, this must be very humiliating for you to handle such a small case?"

"Thank you."

The second case involved me representing a company that was drilling deep under the ground to obtain some soil samples. They accidentally struck and burst open the largest sewer pipe in Orange County, Florida. It was literally a shitshow.

One of the other attorneys on the case, Adam Herman, asked me:

"Ric, what's it like for you to be practicing law again—do you like it?"

"Well, a month ago, I was flying on Air Force One. Now, I'm literally dealing with shit. How do you think I like it?"

Still, I was grateful to have a job.

The second benefit from the election setback was money. Luckily, as a partner in a law firm, I made a lot more money than I did as a congressman. I have five kids to put through college.

The third benefit was more quality time with my family, especially my son and four daughters. Before, in a typical week, I would have to be in Washington from Monday through Thursday for votes, which could cause me to miss some of my children's school plays, basketball games, and dance performances. I'd be back in Orlando for Friday, Saturday, and Sunday, but even then, I was not always fully present because of town hall meetings, constituent meetings, speeches, media, dinner banquets, and other events. Not anymore. I got the chance to be a real parent again.

Setbacks are temporary. It's a part of the process when you are on the road to success. "Failure is a detour, not a dead-end street," said Zig Ziglar.

CHAPTER 7
Focus

"A man who chases two rabbits catches neither."
—Chinese Proverb

One has to stay focused like a laser beam on one definite chief aim to make a huge impact. If you took a piece of notebook paper and placed it on the sidewalk on a summer day, nothing would happen. The sun's rays would scatter across the paper. On the other hand, if you took a magnifying glass and held it there for a period of time on one focal point, the concentrated heat from the energy rays would burn a hole through the paper.

Success is the same way. It requires effort that is focused, concentrated, and persistent. While it is possible to walk and chew gum at the same time, it is exceedingly difficult to have two major competing or conflicting goals at the same time. The old Chinese proverb about the man who chases two rabbits, catching neither, is true. And yet, all too often, people put in huge amounts of effort to try to achieve two big, conflicting goals at once. They have limited or no success and then get frustrated and quit.

Rob Simmons: Standing Firm

Rob Simmons knows a thing or two about the importance of focusing on your goal. Simmons, a Republican from Connecticut, first came to Congress with me in 2000. He was a former CIA agent, had an affable personality, and was good at his job. We occasionally sat together on the House floor.

In May 2005, the Pentagon announced it was closing the Naval Submarine Base in his Connecticut district, which was responsible for 8,500 jobs. It was a big deal. Simmons fought the Pentagon. At one of our weekly, Wednesday-morning, closed-door House GOP conference meetings, I watched as Simmons walked up to the microphone and told the GOP leaders that he wasn't going to be voting their way on any big votes unless and until he got his naval base back. I think some people thought he was kidding. He wasn't.

Shortly thereafter, I happened to be sitting next to Simmons on the House floor, having a conversation during a big, and very close, roll call vote. I had already voted in favor of it. Simmons had not. The Deputy Whip walked over to Simmons and said, "The Speaker asked me to tell you he really needs you to vote yes on this one."

Simmons replied, "Tell the Speaker I'm happy to vote yes—just as soon as I get my f#cking base back." The bold statement caught me off guard and literally made me laugh out loud. If I had been drinking coffee, I would have spit it out. In the majority of cases, the Pentagon and the base realignment and closure officials stand by their original decisions.

Until the Navy base issue was resolved, nothing else mattered to him. He was focused like a laser beam. The Speaker, several power-ful committee chairmen, and many other elected officials eventually rallied behind Simmons. And guess what? He got his freaking base back. It was a huge victory and saved thousands of jobs in his district.

The next year, 2006, those same constituents narrowly voted him out of office in a wave election. Wave elections tend to reflect the overall mood of the country. The downside of wave elections, whether they are Democratic or Republican waves, is that sometimes good people get swept out of office. This was one of those times.

I took two lessons from that experience. First, focused determi-nation makes a difference. Second, you never know what tomorrow will bring, so do the right thing when possible. It's always possible.

The Prince of Al-Qaeda in Iraq[49]

This is the behind-the-scenes story of the incredibly focused effort of General Stanley McChrystal in getting a terrorist named Abu Musab al-Zarqawi ("Zarqawi"). Osama bin Laden called Zarqawi "the Prince of Al-Qaeda in Iraq." Zarqawi always wore black from head to toe. He was the most wanted terrorist in Iraq. The US offered $25 million for any tip that led to his capture. The only other person in the world with a $25-million bounty was Osama bin Laden.

Zarqawi sealed his reputation as an evil monster by personally beheading American hostages. Zarqawi, a Jordanian, was the opera-tional commander of the "Al-Qaeda in Iraq" terrorist group. He bombed the Golden Mosque in Samarra, Iraq; the United Nations headquarters in Baghdad; and three hotels in Amman.

Zarqawi's specialty was creating chaos in Iraq by inciting a civil war between the Sunni and Shia. The conflicts between Shia and Sunni Muslims go back to the death of the Prophet Muhammad in 632 AD. There was a dispute over who should be his successor. The Shia believed that Muhammad's successor should be one of his descendants. The Sunnis didn't believe the leadership of the Muslim world should necessarily pass through hereditary succession.

Zarqawi—a Sunni—found a dramatic way to escalate the division. The Golden Mosque in Samarra, Iraq, nicknamed for its glistening dome, was one of Shiism's holiest sites. On February 22, 2006, the Golden Mosque was destroyed by bombs planted by Zarqawi. Shiites called it their 9/11.

Within hours of the Golden Mosque bombing, spontaneous sectarian violence broke out. Furious Shiites organized militias and went on a methodical, cold-blooded killing spree through Sunni neighborhoods, street by street. Sunni militias, in turn, responded by doing the same thing in Shiite neighborhoods. A thousand Iraqis were killed within five days after the bombing.

After the Golden Mosque bombing, the sectarian warfare nearly took Iraq to the brink of a civil war. I was on the Crime, Terrorism, and Homeland Security subcommittee. I wanted to see what was going on firsthand and meet the guy in charge of hunting down Zarqawi.

I flew to Iraq as part of a six-member congressional delegation. On May 29, 2006, we arrived in Baghdad and got a briefing from Ambassador Zalmay Khalilzad, the US Ambassador to Iraq. We then boarded a Black Hawk helicopter and flew about fifty miles north of Baghdad to the Joint Special Operations Command (JSOC, pronounced "Jay-Sock") in Balad.

The purpose of visiting JSOC was to get a briefing from the guy in charge of taking out Zarqawi. He was a three-star general named Stanley McChrystal. We began by touring the JSOC center, where I noticed several posters of Zarqawi on the walls. It was clear from the surroundings that the key focus was getting Zarqawi.

General McChrystal then gave us a detailed briefing regarding the search for Zarqawi. He was confident and optimistic. I asked him, "General, are you going to get Zarqawi?" He replied, "I have no doubt. We are very close right now. We're going to get him." I believed him. General McChrystal was focused and projected confidence. It was justified. In fact, even while we were being briefed that day (May 29, 2006), his elite JSOC team was using a drone to track the man who would lead them to Zarqawi.

General McChrystal wrote about it in his memoir, *My Share of the Task*. About ten days before our visit, on May 18, an Iraqi detainee gave McChrystal's team the name and home address of Zarqawi's spiritual adviser, Sheik Abd al-Rahman. Rahman regularly met with Zarqawi every seven to ten days. The JSOC team was monitoring Rahman's every move around the clock via reconnaissance drones. It was just a matter of time. But when would we find out?

Fast forward about a week later. I was back in America. It was the afternoon of Wednesday, June 7, 2006, and I was attending a meeting at the White House to brief President George W. Bush about our recent trip to Iraq. Also sitting at the table with President Bush and me were Vice President Dick Cheney, Secretary of State Condoleezza Rice, National Security Advisor Stephen Hadley, Senator Elizabeth Dole, and Congressmen Roy Blunt, Jeff Miller, and Ray LaHood.

The meeting started at about 3:30 PM. Stephen Hadley was sitting near me. I noticed he kept fiddling around with his BlackBerry. After about fifteen minutes, at around 3:45 PM, Hadley got up and left the room. I thought to myself, *That's odd. Why would a White House staff member walk out of a meeting with the president and vice president?*

What could be so important? When Hadley returned, he whispered something in President Bush's ear and then slipped a note to Secretary Rice. After Rice read the note, Bush winked at her. I'll never forget that wink.

My instinct told me something big had just happened. I made a note of the time: "3:57 PM, 6/7/06, WH." President Bush was tight-lipped the rest of the day. My hunch was right. On the following day at 7:31 AM, Thursday, June 8, 2006, President Bush strolled into the Rose Garden and made a blockbuster announcement:

"United States military forces killed the terrorist Zarqawi."

What had happened in the last twenty-four hours? McChrystal's JSOC crew had tracked the spiritual adviser, Rahman, via drone as he traveled north on the road from Baghdad to a small village called Hibhib. The adviser then entered a boxy, two-story home surrounded by palm trees.

Shortly thereafter, a man—dressed in black from head to toe—walked out of the house and down the driveway toward the road. Once at the road, he looked left, looked right, and then walked back to the house. The drone captured it on video. "That's Zarqawi," said General McChrystal.

McChrystal immediately approved the order for an F-16 fighter jet to drop two five-hundred-pound bombs on the house. The massive bombs struck their target and turned the house into a pile of rubble. Zarqawi's body was then taken back to JSOC headquarters in Balad, where General McChrystal personally confirmed his identity through scars, tattoos, and facial features.

What had happened during our White House meeting the day before? When Hadley had stepped out of the room, it was to take a call from Ambassador Khalilzad—the guy I had met with in Baghdad a week earlier. The ambassador told him that McChrystal's team had just killed Zarqawi. At the time, they were still waiting on the FBI to confirm the fingerprints. Later that night, the prints were confirmed to be a 100 percent match for Zarqawi. By the following morning, President Bush was ready to make the announcement. The "Prince of Al-Qaeda in Iraq" would never murder again.

Meanwhile, another focused manhunt was underway that would attract even more attention.

America Versus Osama bin Laden[50]

The ten-year manhunt for Osama bin Laden is another example of focused effort and preparation. On Tuesday, September 11, 2001, I walked to my Capitol Hill office while others made their way to work at the Pentagon, and in New York, many people headed to their jobs at the World Trade Center. I'm sure you remember where you were on September 11, 2001. The country singer Alan Jackson captured the emotions felt by many Americans on September 11 in his Grammy Award-winning song, "Where Were You (When the World Stopped Turning)."

On September 14, 2001, President George W. Bush stood at Ground Zero, where the Twin Towers of the World Trade Center were still smoldering. The president climbed on top of some rubble, grabbed a bullhorn, and started thanking the firefighters and other first responders at the scene. A rescue worker shouted, "I can't hear you." President Bush spontaneously replied with the words that made history: "I can hear you! The rest of the world hears you! And the people—and the people who knocked these buildings down will hear all of us soon." The crowd reacted with loud, prolonged chants of "USA! USA! USA!"

Five years passed, and we still hadn't found him. On May 30, 2006, I traveled to Islamabad, Pakistan, as part of a six-person congressional delegation to meet with President Pervez Musharraf. After we exchanged pleasantries, I asked Musharraf some questions:

Me: "Mr. President, are you actively and specifically looking for Osama bin Laden?"

Musharraf: "Honestly, no. Specifically looking for him? No."

I had a really bad feeling about Musharraf. My intuition told me that Osama bin Laden was in Pakistan, that the Pakistan intelligence officials were helping him, and that if we developed any actionable intelligence regarding his location, we should not compromise it by sharing it with Pakistan in advance. I documented these thoughts in a June 7, 2006, memorandum titled "Search for Osama bin Laden" that I sent to the White House. The director of national intelligence, John Negroponte, wrote me back and told me he had forwarded my memorandum to the CIA Counterterrorism Center.

My instincts turned out to be right. We would later learn that while I was meeting with Musharraf in Islamabad, Pakistan, on May 29, 2006, not only was Osama bin Laden living in Pakistan, but he was only thirty miles away. He was living in a large compound in Abbottabad, about a half-mile from Pakistan's version of West Point military academy. Bin Laden's wife later confirmed that bin Laden had been living in Abbottabad since 2005. I wasn't surprised at all when he was found where he was, though I certainly didn't have his address.

Wisely, President Obama and the CIA did not give Pakistani intelligence officials any advance warning before the SEAL Team Six raid. Leon Panetta, Obama's CIA chief, told *Time* magazine on May 3, 2011, that "It was decided that any effort to work with the Pakistanis could jeopardize the mission. They might alert the targets," Panetta said.

The sequence of events started in August 2001, when an astute immigration inspector at Orlando International Airport stopped the intended twentieth hijacker, Mohammed al-Qahtani ("Qahtani"), from entering the United States. (See Chapter 3. After being sent home, Qahtani was captured along the Afghanistan-Pakistan border and sent to Guantanamo Bay, Cuba. In 2003, Qahtani, during interrogation, identified Abu Ahmed al-Kuwaiti—"the Kuwaiti"—who was bin Laden's courier.)

The trail went cold until 2007 when the CIA learned the Kuwaiti's real name, Ibrahim Saeed Ahmed. Before that, the Kuwaiti had used multiple aliases, and only a handful of family and close friends knew his real name.

In June 2010, the Kuwaiti made changes in the way he communicated via cell phone that made it possible to use geolocation technology to track his phone. In August 2010, the CIA tracked the Kuwaiti to the city of Peshawar, Pakistan, and the Kuwaiti's distinctive white Suzuki SUV (with a rhino spare tire cover) allowed the CIA to follow the courier to bin Laden's home in Abbottabad. In April 2011, President Obama approved the raid.

On May 2, 2011, SEAL Team Six successfully raided the Abbottabad compound and killed bin Laden. After President Obama received word that SEAL Team Six's raid had successfully captured and killed Osama bin Laden, his first call was to President George W. Bush. It was fitting. It made me proud of both men. As Obama later said, making his first call to his predecessor was an "important symbol" that while we may get into partisan fights, at the end of the day, we are all Americans. Later that same night, it was the top of the ninth inning between the New York Mets and the Philadelphia Phillies, and the score was tied, when the 45,000 fans at Philadelphia's stadium heard the breaking news that Osama bin Laden had finally been killed.

All of a sudden, 45,000 fans erupted with sustained chants of "USA! USA! USA!" The chants went on so long that the game was delayed. It didn't matter anymore what team they were rooting for that night. Everyone was on the same team.

We still are.

Tale of the Tape

The man who formulated and executed the plan that brought Osama bin Laden to justice is Admiral William McRaven. The SEAL Team Six raid that killed bin Laden has ensured McRaven's place in the history books as the architect of the operation.

During the spring of 2011, McRaven created the plan for the assault on the compound in Abbottabad, Pakistan, where bin Laden was believed to be hiding. The tricky part was the issue of Pakistan's sovereignty—the compound was 150 miles inside Pakistan—and making sure the SEAL Team Six crew returned safely to Afghanistan after its mission. After repeated rehearsals of the raid in both North Carolina and Nevada that included a full-scale model of the compound bin Laden was believed to be hiding in, McRaven went to the White House to advise Obama that his men would be able to execute the mission successfully. President Obama approved the raid.

Just before the mission, McRaven gathered his SEAL team together and shared the movie *Hoosiers* as an analogy.[51] In the movie, actor Gene Hackman plays Coach Norman Dale. To get his small-town team prepared to play for the state championship, which was in the big arena, the coach pulled out a tape measure and had the players measure the distance from the basket to the floor to demonstrate that it was ten feet, just like in the gym where they practiced every day.

Even though the mission they were about to do would make history, McRaven channeled his inner Coach Dale and said, "All of you have been on hundreds of missions. Just do this mission the way you have done every other mission, and we'll be just fine. Another night, another raid."

McRaven then ran the mission from his command post in Afghanistan. On the night of May 1, 2011, as the president and his national security team monitored from the White House, McRaven calmly gave progress updates to the president in a cool-as-a-cucumber manner, even when one of the helicopters went down inside the compound.

After the SEALs captured and killed bin Laden, they brought the body back. McRaven personally inspected the body to make sure that it was bin Laden. McRaven knew bin Laden was about six foot four, but he didn't have a tape measure. So McRaven asked a young SEAL who was six foot two to lie down next to the body, and that was good enough.

When McRaven told Obama the news, he apologized for the downed stealth helicopter and joked, "Well, sir, I guess I owe you $60 million." Obama shot back, "Let me get this straight, Bill. I just lost a $60 million helicopter in Pakistan, and you don't have $1.99 for a tape measure?"

A few days later, President Obama invited Admiral McRaven to the White House and presented the admiral with a Home Depot tape measure attached to a plaque.

Three years later, McRaven gave a memorable Make Your Bed commencement speech to the graduating class at the University of Texas which went viral. McRaven suggested that changing the world for the better is possible and it starts with making your bed. Humbly, McRaven's commencement address did not even mention the SEAL Team Six raid which killed bin Laden. The speech was later turned into a book by the same name which became a number-one *New York Times* bestseller. In short, because of McRaven's contributions, we sleep better at night and make our beds in the morning. That's a pretty amazing legacy by any tape measure.

Focus is the key. Don't worry about getting more things done. Use your energy to get the right thing done. When you are finished with the book, please go back and reread Chapter 2 carefully. There is nothing so powerful as the three-step formula to keep you laser focused on achieving your mission.

TAKEAWAY

Maintain focused and concentrated effort on one major goal at a time. Don't chase two rabbits. Get the *right* thing done, not *more* things done.

part TWO

CONNECTING
WITH PEOPLE

CHAPTER 8
Connecting the Dots

"You can't connect the dots looking forward;
you can only connect them looking backwards."
—Steve Jobs

You are planting seeds today that will reap significant benefits years down the road. You can't connect the dots looking forward. However, if you live authentically, use your gifts, and trust your intuition, then one day you will look back and see how seemingly unrelated actions will come together in a way that makes sense. You'll see that your so-called "failures" and heartbreaks were the best things that could have happened to you because God had something better planned for you than you had for yourself.

For now, it is important for you to live authentically and trust that the dots will connect. This will give you the confidence to trust your intuition even when it leads you down an unconventional path. We are all connected. The Universe is incredibly good at connecting you with the people and events you need for your mission.

Resurrecting the Big Tree[52]

When I was about ten years old, my mom went to work as a secretary for R.T. Overstreet, the president of Overstreet Investment Company. He is the kind-hearted elderly man who helped pay for my college education. Mr. Overstreet's father, State Senator Moses Overstreet, also had a charitable spirit. In 1927, Senator Overstreet donated a tract of land to Seminole County to create a public park in Longwood, Florida, called Big Tree Park (near Orlando).

Big Tree Park, dedicated by President Calvin Coolidge in 1929, got its name because it was home to the largest and oldest bald cypress tree in the United States, named "the Senator" in honor of the donor. The Senator stood 125 feet high, 18 feet wide, and was 3,500 years old, making it the fifth-oldest tree in the world. It was a popular destination for schoolchildren in Central Florida, and my mom took me to Big Tree Park dozens of times.

On a cold night, January 16, 2012, a twenty-six-year-old female drug addict snuck into Big Tree Park and lit a fire inside the Senator while smoking methamphetamine. The fire quickly grew out of control, raged for hours, and destroyed the majestic tree. Instead of calling the fire department, she took photographs of the tree as it burned and showed them to others, exclaiming, "I can't believe I burned down a tree older than Jesus."[53] She was arrested, convicted, and sent to prison for thirty months.

The entire Central Florida community was shocked. I shed a few tears myself. Shortly after the fire, Paul Peterzell of Longwood, Florida, summed up the feelings of so many with his poignant poem:

An Ode to the Big Tree[54]

A place where people gathered,
traveled far and wide,
Witnessing a marvel,
Suddenly it died.

Over 3,500 years old,
towering above it all,
One early January morning,
they sadly watched it fall.

Named for a Senator,
dedicated by a president,
It wasn't until now,
that I realize what it meant.

For years the main attraction,
delighted at the site,
Walking away in amazement,
its grandeur and its might!

I heard of the fire,
as I shed some tears,
How could this happen,
after so many happy years?

Millions were in awe,
generations came to see
How one sad day in history,
A fire destroyed this tree.

A park's namesake indeed,
Such beauty all around,
The "Senator" will be missed,
no replacement can be found.

> As we pause and think,
> how much this tree had meant,
> 3,500 years have gone by
> beautiful time spent.
>
> Big Tree Park remains,
> Memories will take hold.
> A cypress oh so famous,
> another story told.

Unbeknownst to the poet, there was a chance that "a replacement [could] be found." Sixteen years before the fire, a high school science teacher from Miami, named Layman Hardy, happened to be visiting Big Tree Park the day after a storm, which caused a branch of the Senator to break off and fall to the ground. The branch had small buds on it, the key to cloning a tree.

Following his instincts, the science teacher picked up the branch and delivered it to a North Florida nursery owner, Marvin Buchanan, who had been working with some University of Florida forestry genetics researchers, including Don Rockwood, on a cypress tree cloning experiment.

Cloning a tree is hard. The odds of it working are very slim. First, you have to graft a bud onto the roots of other cypress trees. Second, after the tiny trees begin to spring up, they have to be transplanted to sink roots of their own. Third, the little trees must survive disease, storms, and hurricanes. Ninety percent will not survive.

In this case, after sixteen years elapsed, many of the researchers involved with the project had moved on, and the cloning of the Senator became a forgotten experiment.

In August 2012—about eight months after the fire—Buchanan's phone rang with an unusual request. The Seminole County officials wanted to know: (1) if the cloning experiment using the Senator's buds had worked and (2), if so, where was the Senator's cloned tree located?

The answer was YES, the experiment had worked! The Senator's cloning material had extraordinarily strong characteristics, and the sturdy replacement was rapidly growing at the rate of about three feet a year and had already reached fifty feet in height. The tree, a 100 percent clone of the Senator, was still located on Buchanan's property, about 185 miles north of Big Tree Park.

The Seminole County officials were excited and purchased the tree. This led to the difficult challenge of figuring out how to move the mighty tree to Big Tree Park. Buchanan's crew began digging. It took six months to prepare a tree the size of the Senator's replacement for transplant. The roots were spread out dozens of feet and had to be surgically extracted from the soil without harming the tree. The transport of the tree was also a massive undertaking that ultimately required a crane and a heavy-duty tractor-trailer able to bear the tree's weight.

But they did it! The Senator's replacement was successfully transported and transplanted into Big Tree Park.

The next task was naming the tree. Local officials held a contest and invited local schoolchildren to submit their suggestions. The winner was a fourth-grader named May Frangoul, who came up with the perfect name, "the Phoenix." The elementary school student said, "Since the Phoenix is a mythical bird that rises out of the ashes, I thought it would be good for the tree since it got burned down and now there's a new one they got planted."

The Phoenix now stands tall in Big Tree Park and is growing every day. Buchanan, the nursery grower, said: "It was just pure old luck of the draw, or Providence. God has a hand in everything. I assume he had a hand in this as well."

Standing next to the Phoenix, miraculous descendant of the Senator, a decade after the ancient tree's destruction.

There are at least three lessons that we can draw from this miraculous story.

First, you are planting seeds now that you will reap later in ways you can't imagine, short term and long term. It may not make sense now, but in the future, you will look back on your life and see how the dots connect. Seemingly unrelated actions will come together in a way that makes sense. If you believe that the dots will connect down the road, it will give you the confidence to trust your intuition even when it leads you down an unconventional path.

You must be open-minded when your intuition calls you to act in certain ways. There may be actions your gut tells you to take that don't make sense or seem connected at all with what you are trying to achieve—take those actions anyway.

The immortal Ralph Waldo Emerson said in his essay on "Self-Reliance:"

"There will be an agreement in whatever variety of actions, so they be each honest and natural in their hour. For of one will, the actions will be harmonious, however unlikely they seem. These varieties are lost sight of at a little distance, at a little height of thought. One tendency unites them all. The voyage of the best ship is a zigzag line of a hundred tacks. See the line from a sufficient distance, and it will straighten itself to the average tendency. Your genuine action will explain itself and will explain your other genuine actions . . . Be it how it will, do right now."

Be patient—not everything you do today will have an immediate positive impact; you may have to wait years or even decades for the tiny seed to flourish. It may be that your small action today does not help you personally but instead will have a huge positive impact on another person or situation that you don't even know about. Who knew that a science teacher's intuition to pick up a fallen tree branch would end up giving rebirth to a 3,500-year-old tree two decades later? But it did.

The second lesson is not to let the challenges ahead deter you. Many people discourage themselves from even starting: "There's no way I'll get into that college; only one in ten people get in." "There's no way I'll get that job; it's very selective." But if your gut is telling you to go for something, you should do it. The Universe is phenomenally good at aligning the people, resources, and events to bring about the desired outcome.

So many improbable steps had to go right for the Senator to be reborn as the Phoenix. A storm had to knock a branch off the Senator; the branch had to have buds on it; a science teacher had to see it, pick it up, and know where to deliver it; a team of university researchers had to assist with a difficult cloning procedure; a farmer had to be willing to take a risk even though there was only a 10 percent chance of success; and the little replacement tree Phoenix would have to be incredibly strong to survive sixteen years of storms, hurricanes, disease, and a highly complex surgical transplantation and transportation process. Any one of these prior steps could have gone horribly wrong, but it didn't. Against all odds, it was successful.

Therefore, next time your intuition is screaming at you to take a chance on your dreams, instead of being fearful about all the things that could go wrong, why not ask yourself, *What if it all goes right? What if it all works out? What if the stars line up?* If the Universe can make a tree rise from the ashes, it can help you, too.

Third, an important lesson is resilience during a catastrophe. The burning of the 3,500-year-old tree was a horrific tragedy. But against all odds, a replacement was found. Many of the tragedies we face seem similarly impossible to survive. We fail out of college, we get fired from a job, a friend betrays us, our marriage collapses, etc. But often, those setbacks lead us in a new direction, to new opportunities that we would not have explored otherwise, to better or revised plans, to self-improvement, or to the discovery or utilization of our God-given gifts.

Lisa Kudrow: Following the Friendly Guideposts[55]

Lisa Kudrow, the actress from the hit TV show *Friends*, was a biology major at Vassar College. She never had anything to do with acting in high school or at Vassar. She had never been in a play. Six months after her college graduation, at twenty-two, her intuition told her to become an actress. She didn't yet know why, but "I just listened to that inner voice."

She began by taking improv classes at The Groundlings, an

improvisation and sketch comedy theater in LA. On her first day, she met Conan O'Brien. She thought Conan was exceptionally talented. The fact that Conan thought she was funny, too, gave her confidence to believe that she belonged in the acting profession.

Kudrow's hopes soared after she quickly landed a small part in a play. She was cast in the TV pilot for *Romy and Michele,* based on the play. She was crushed when the pilot didn't get picked up, and she was back to square one.

Over the next eight years, Kudrow's resolve and confidence were tested. Casting directors told her that she was not pretty enough or talented enough. After years of improv classes, Kudrow finally landed a coveted spot in the main company of The Groundlings—the same place where *Saturday Night Live* stars Will Ferrell, Kristen Wiig, and Phil Hartman were discovered. One night when she was performing, Lorne Michaels, SNL's creator and producer, came to a show at The Groundlings to look for new cast members. He picked her colleague Julia Sweeney, and Kudrow was devastated. She was knocked off balance and began to question if she even belonged in acting.

And then she got cast as a regular on the hit show *Frasier.* She thought she had finally made it. But after two days of rehearsal, she got fired from *Frasier* and replaced by actress Peri Gilpin. Kudrow was broke and brokenhearted and thought about quitting the business.

A couple of months later, she was offered a temporary bit part playing a waitress on the show *Mad About You.* It was such a small role that her agent recommended she pass on it. She did the guest appearance anyway, and through that show, met a contact who asked her to come in to read for his new show about six twenty-somethings who lived in New York City and hung out at a coffee house. She got the part. The show was called *Friends.* The hit show was on the air for ten years, and Lisa Kudrow won an Emmy Award for Outstanding Supporting Actress in a Comedy Series.

Years later, Kudrow was able to look back on all those setbacks and realize how lucky she was to get fired from *Frasier*, rejected by *SNL*, and disappointed by the *Romy and Michele* pilot not being picked up. If those things hadn't happened, she wouldn't have landed *Friends*.

In her inspirational commencement address at her alma mater Vassar, Kudrow said that these setbacks were like guideposts that kept her on her true path, both professionally and personally:

> "After I got fired from *Frasier*, I went to a birthday party and, feeling like I had nothing at all to lose, I flirted with a guy who was way out of my league. We dated, and on Thursday, Michel and I will have been married for fifteen years. Yeah, that's the biggest achievement of all, and we'll be celebrating with our twelve-year-old son. Thank God I got fired! Maybe there is a reason for everything. I think there is."

In your life, you'll look backward and see that the reason you went through those so-called "failures" is that the Universe had much better plans for you than you had for yourself. What you thought were setbacks were actually friendly guideposts to guide you back to your true path.

Steve Jobs: Calligraphy Goes High-Tech[56]

Steve Jobs dropped out of college after the first six months. The required college courses didn't interest him, but his intuition told him to hang around campus for a while to take an elective calligraphy class. He loved learning about what makes great typography, including the importance of spacing between different letter combinations and the serif and sans-serif typefaces.

At the time, none of these newfound calligraphy skills had any practical application in his life. But ten years later, when the Apple cofounder and CEO was designing the first Macintosh computer, it all came back to him. He designed the Mac to be the first computer with beautiful typography, including multiple typefaces and proportionally spaced fonts. If this had not happened, personal computers might not have the wonderful typography they have today.

Many years later, Jobs gave a moving commencement address at Stanford. He said following his intuition to drop out of college and drop in on this calligraphy class was one of the best decisions he ever made, and later, he was able to "connect the dots":

> "Of course, it was impossible to connect the dots looking forward when I was in college. But it was very, very clear looking backwards ten years later. . . . You can't connect the dots looking forward; you can only connect them looking backwards. So you have to trust that the dots will somehow connect in your future. You have to trust in something—your gut, destiny, life, karma, whatever. Because believing that the dots will connect down the road will give you the confidence to follow your heart even when it leads you off the well-worn path and that will make all the difference. . . . Don't let the noise of others' opinions drown out your own inner voice. And most important, have the courage to follow your heart and intuition. They somehow already know what you truly want to become."

Six Degrees of Kevin Bacon

We are all connected. "Six Degrees of Separation" is the concept that everyone on the planet is connected to each other by no more than six others. The concept was popularized by the game Six Degrees of Kevin Bacon. The premise is that anyone in the Hollywood film industry can be linked through their roles to Kevin Bacon within six steps (and typically fewer). For example, Elvis Presley was in the movie *Change of Habit* (1969) with Ed Asner. Ed Asner was in the movie *JFK* (1991) with Kevin Bacon.

Here's another little example. I sponsored legislation to protect the movie industry from piracy, and the president of the Motion Picture Association of America testified on behalf of my bill. I was elected to Congress at the same time as Congressman Ander Crenshaw (R-FL) from Jacksonville. I met one of Crenshaw's staff members, named Liam Lynch. Lynch moved to New York City and heads a venture capital group. Lynch was kind enough to invite me to stay at his home on a business trip. The home had a beautiful open-air rooftop patio and views of NYC. I asked him how he got such a cool house. He bought it from Kevin Bacon.

Here's the point. Whether it's Colonel Sanders and Dave Thomas or Elvis Presley and Kevin Bacon, we are all connected. That is why the Universe has more than enough power to connect you with the people and events who can help you get from where you are to where you want to be. When you finish this book, go back and reread Chapter 2 and harness the power of the three-step success formula.

The Failed Job

Every setback carries with it a lesson or blessing, but sometimes you've got to wait on both of them. Eventually, when you look back, you will see how all the dots connect and that your "failure" really was a blessing in disguise.

For example, when I graduated from Vanderbilt Law School, I went to work as an attorney at the Lowndes Law Firm in Orlando. At the time, it was the largest firm based in Orlando, had a prestigious reputation, and paid well. I had done my summer clerkship there between my second and third year of law school, and they gave me an offer and a lucrative signing bonus. I accepted.

My natural gifts of speaking and writing make litigation and trial work relatively easy for me. However, instead, they had me doing many real estate closings and residential foreclosures. I found real estate law to be very boring, and I didn't like kicking people out of their homes. I was miserable. I don't have anything bad to say about the firm, but the type of work wasn't a good fit for me. Since I hated my day job, I used my free time doing things that gave me joy, including mentoring at-risk students and writing jokes for Jeb Bush's first campaign for governor of Florida.

With Florida Governor Jeb Bush and President George W. Bush at the Orlando Airport tarmac.

After less than two years, I switched to a big firm that did strictly litigation, called Rumberger, Kirk & Caldwell, and my job happiness went from a two to a nine on a scale of one to ten. They liked me, promoted me to partner, and generously donated to my campaign.

I felt like I had wasted two years of my life at the prior firm. Eight years later, God would finally reveal to me four different blessings from my Lowndes experience. First, my opponent in my first race for Congress in 2000 was Linda Chapin, who had been the mayor of Orange County. Her campaign manager was the wife of one of the Lowndes senior partners. In other words, if I had stayed at that firm, they never would have supported me running for Congress.

Second, I got to be friends with one of the partners, former Congressman Lou Frey, who had a great sense of humor. I got the Elizabeth Taylor wedding-night joke from him, which took me from an underfunded, unknown, underdog candidate to the Republican frontrunner and eventual victor on election night. If that line were the only thing I got out of those two miserable years, it would have been worth it.

Third, Governor Bush was very popular in Florida when I ran in 2000. Many other elected officials began endorsing my primary opponent, especially when I came in a distant second in the primary. Not Jeb. I e-mailed him and reminded him of my early support—and self-deprecating joke—that I gave him in his first race. He agreed to stay out of the primary and then personally came to Orlando with Senator John McCain to do a campaign rally for me on the day before my general election.

Fourth, when I was doing the COMPACT Mentoring program in Orlando—where I personally mentored two students at my alma mater, Boone High School, and gave fifty speeches in the community to recruit seven hundred mentors—Nebraska football coach Tom Osborne had started a mentoring program in Nebraska at the same time. As luck would have it, Osborne got elected to Congress the same day as me and sat next to me on the Education Committee. Based on our shared experiences, we coauthored the Mentoring for Success Act signed into law by President George W. Bush as part of his education reform legislation.

I thought it had been a miserable job failure, but years later, all of the dots connected to show me that this failure allowed me to run for Congress, raise $400,000, get the governor's help, and pass mentoring legislation. It was the best thing that could have happened to me.

Connecting the Dots in Your Personal Life

One day all of the dots will connect with your personal life as well as your work life. Many years from now, you will look back and see that the reason you experienced some romantic heartbreaks is because God had something better planned for you than you had for yourself.

One of the most common causes of failure is the wrong selection of a mate in marriage. I've heard some people say, "Marriage is hard work." To be sure, life is not always rainbows and butterflies. However, marriage shouldn't be *that* hard. Harmony between two people in an intimate relationship should be easy, not hard. When you are with the right person, it should feel like paddling downstream. One of the most soul-crushing things is staying in a toxic relationship that is marked by misery and unhappiness. You deserve better. Don't settle.

You can't connect the dots looking forward, so the best thing you can do now is to live authentically, trust your intuition, and err on the side of self-respect by making big decisions in your personal life based upon what makes you feel better about yourself.

I don't approach this topic from a high and mighty perspective as someone who has always got it right in the past. By the end of 2018, I had lost an election, had two failed marriages, and my energy was sapped from working long hours at the law firm. I felt drained by life.

Everything in my life changed on February 28, 2019. A buddy named Jason was kicking off his campaign for public office. Since the venue was only a mile from my home, I planned to stop by for a few minutes after work. After the official event, a small group of us went to a nearby Irish pub, including a few of Jason's friends from his college days at the University of Florida. One of them was Lori.

Lori was beautiful, bright, and kindhearted. She had been Homecoming Queen at the University of Florida, got her MBA from Harvard, and ran a nonprofit foundation focused on reducing poverty in Africa. She was also witty and had a positive energy about her. I was smitten.

We started dating right away. About two months later, I took Lori to see a Chicago tribute band concert near our hometown of Orlando. Our favorite Chicago song was called "Just You 'N' Me." It was the first time we said "I love you" to each other.

Fast forward six months. It was Lori's birthday. The date was October 19, 2019. As luck would have it, the real Chicago band was playing that night at the Clearwater Jazz Festival, which is only about an hour-and-a-half away from where we live.

I secretly got tickets and kept our destination a surprise until about an hour before the concert. Now what I didn't tell Lori was that I had an engagement ring in my pocket and was going to propose to her at the Chicago concert. For sentimental reasons, my plan was to propose to her while slow dancing to "Just You 'N' Me."

Oh, crap, I thought when we arrived at the venue, and I noticed the metal detectors at the entrance to this outdoor music festival. "Please remove everything from your pockets and put them in the tray," said the security guard. I didn't want her to see the ring. I said, "Hey, Lori, why don't you go through a different metal detector, so we get through faster." And she did. Whew! Crisis averted.

We'd brought our lawn chairs but there was no space left to set them up. I had no idea how popular this event was. Apparently, thousands of people had been camped out since early that morning to get seats for this nighttime concert. We walked up and down looking for a space for about fifteen minutes without any success.

Luckily, a concertgoer named Terry noticed our dilemma and motioned for us to come over. Terry and his buddy had amazing seats near the front of the stage. They were Good Samaritans who could tell we needed help and had squeezed together to make room. Terry even moved his chair to the row just behind us so we could all fit—an incredibly kind gesture from a stranger.

Just before the concert started, Lori walked away for a moment to get a beverage. I took that opportunity to ask for Terry's help. I said, "I'm going to propose to her later in the concert, when they play the song 'Just You 'N' Me.' If I give you my iPhone, would you do me a huge favor and record it on video?" Terry replied, "Of course, man. Happy to do it."

About halfway through the concert, they still hadn't played the song. I felt a tap on my right shoulder. Terry leaned in and whispered, "Hey, man, is this thing still going down?" I laughed and confirmed, "Yes, it's still going down. I think they play the song toward the end."

And then, a few songs later, I felt a chill as the familiar opening horns of "Just You 'N' Me" began to play, and they sang the opening lyrics. Up until that moment, I felt confident and relaxed. No more. Suddenly, I felt really nervous. Life comes down to a few special moments, and it hit me that this was one of them.

I quietly slipped my iPhone behind my back to Terry. Maybe my hand was shaking or something, but I think Terry could sense I was nervous. He put his hand on my right shoulder, leaned forward and whispered, "You got this, buddy. It's going to go great."

I asked Lori to slow dance to our song. About halfway through the song, I got down on one knee and put my hand in the front pocket of my pants to begin to pull out the ring box. Lori didn't know what was going on and asked, "What are you doing?" as she got down on her knees with me. I opened the box, presented the engagement ring, and asked, "Will you marry me?"

She said, "Yes! Yes! Yes!"

Unbeknownst to us, the crowd had figured out what was happening and erupted in applause after she said, "Yes." Like a seasoned Hollywood director, Terry captured everything on video: the slow dance, the band, a close-up of the ring, Lori's face the moment she said, "Yes," and the crowd cheering. It was perfect. Terry had been kind enough to make sure we had great seats near the stage, encourage me when I was nervous, and capture it all on video like a pro.

The Universe will conspire to help you by bringing the right people into your life at the right time, when you are ready for it. It felt like Terry was an angel sent by God to help things go smoothly.

Fast forward to February 28, 2020. Lori and I got married exactly one year to the date after we met. Jason, the mutual friend who introduced us on February 28, 2019, performed the wedding ceremony. He surprised us by incorporating some of the lyrics of "Just You 'N' Me" into the wedding vows. And, to bring things full circle, we got married in the Baldwin Park neighborhood in Orlando, the site of our first date. From February 28 to February 28, Jason to Jason, Chicago to Chicago, Baldwin Park to Baldwin Park. Finally, I could see how all the dots connected in my personal life.

There was one thing I regret. In the excitement of the engagement, I forgot to ask Terry for his card, phone number, or even last name. Lori and I really want to give Terry a big gift certificate to a fancy local steakhouse as a way of saying, "Thank you."

Since we got married, Lori and I have been to about a half-dozen concerts near the area where we got engaged, including one additional Chicago concert. Every single time, Lori looks around the crowd and says, "I wonder if Terry is here." We're still looking. I hope we find him someday.

Christmas 2021 in the Keller home with our big, beautiful blended family.

Connecting the Dots to Write This Book

Connection #1

My father gave me a copy of *Think and Grow Rich* when I was fourteen years old, and it changed my life. When my daughter Kaylee turned fourteen last year, I gave her a copy of *Think and Grow Rich* and thought she would love it.

She said, "Sorry, Dad, I know you love this book, but I just can't get into it. I tried to read a couple of chapters. It's all about these old men trying to get rich. And there's no 'girl power' stories. I can't relate to it."

My first reaction was disappointment. Personally, I think *Think and Grow Rich* is the greatest self-help book of all time, and the lessons are timeless.

But I tried to understand her point of view. Yes, this book was written during the Great Depression in 1937 and does mostly talk about making money. Hill wrote, "The major reason why I wrote this book on how to get money is the fact that millions of men and women are paralyzed with the fear of poverty." And, yes, the book does tell the stories of older men from the past century, such as Andrew Carnegie, Henry Ford, and Thomas Edison.

It occurred to me to write something that Kaylee and her peers would read. My thoughts were to: (1) use lots of modern-day stories and current celebrities, (2) include lots of detailed "girl power" stories (such as Abby Wambach, Lisa Kudrow, Dolly Parton, Jamie Kern Lima, Lori Keller, and Oprah Winfrey), (3) give examples of the famous goal-setting formula being applied to other goals beyond financial, such as getting good grades, becoming CEO of a business or nonprofit organization, becoming a famous actress or singer, winning an election, losing weight, or earning a gold medal, and (4) use some humor and easy-to-read stories to make it fun.

I sent a couple of sample chapters to Kaylee that included those four things. She replied, "OMG!! I love it!! I'm not just saying that!!"

Connection #2

I asked my wife for her thoughts. Lori said, "You have enough achievements to be credible, failures to be relatable, and humor to make it entertaining. You should do it."

Connection #3

Napoleon Hill and I do have some crazy coincidences. We were born within a few miles of each other, Napoleon Hill in Wise County, Virginia; me in Johnson City, Tennessee.

Napoleon Hill gave a graduation speech that inspired a young man to run for Congress; I read about that story in *Think and Grow Rich*, and it inspired me to run for Congress.

Napoleon Hill used the money from *Think and Grow Rich* to buy a mansion in Mt. Dora, Florida; I got elected to Congress and represented Mt. Dora, Florida.

The Napoleon Hill Foundation CEO, Don Green, is the one who introduced me to my literary agent.

Don Green was born in Johnson City, Tennessee. Ditto. Don graduated from ETSU. Me, too. Don lives in Wise County, Virginia—the birthplace of Napoleon Hill.

TAKEAWAY

It is impossible to connect the dots looking forward,
but believe they will connect someday. Rest assured,
the little seeds that you are planting today along your
journey will one day have a significant benefit to
you or others down the road.

For now, your mission is to live authentically,
use your gifts, and trust your intuition enough to take
those bold little steps that are aligned with your
purpose. If you do that, when you look backward,
it will be clear how all of the dots connect. Of course,
that is why it is possible for you today to pull out
your iPhone and use it to snap a photo of the
Phoenix or watch an episode of *Friends.*

When you're feeling down and out, realize that
things are not as bad as they seem. There are angels
all around us, and they're on the side of
big trees and big dreams.

CHAPTER 9

The Secret Power of Self-Deprecating Humor

"Laugh at yourself and at life, and nothing can touch you."
—Louise Hay

Self-deprecating humor is a secret weapon. It relaxes people, deflects criticism, and builds rapport. Why do so few people use it? Because, for many people, it is *counterintuitive*. From an early age, we've been encouraged to present a perfect image to the outside world in order to be successful in life. "Fake it till you make it." "Put your best foot forward." "Never let them see you sweat."

The truth is exactly the *opposite* of all that advice. The *truth* is that to connect with people, you have to be authentic, vulnerable, and real.

It takes self-confidence to use self-deprecating humor. It essentially says, "Look, I *know* I'm flawed. But I also know that I'm a good person, I believe in myself, and you should, too."

Research Studies Prove It

And the studies show that it works: in politics, in business, and in life.

Researchers from East Carolina University looked at the power of self-deprecating humor in politics.[57] Chris Christie, the former New Jersey governor, ran for president in 2016. The researchers showed one group of people a video of David Letterman reading a Top Ten list where he made fun of Christie with a bunch of fat jokes. I've struggled with weight my whole life, so I didn't really care for it.

The researchers then showed a second group of people a different video clip. This video was of Chris Christie personally appearing as a guest on the *Late Show with David Letterman*. During Letterman's interview of him, Christie made fun of himself by pulling out a donut and starting to eat it. He said, "I didn't know this was going to be this long."

The people who saw Christie poking fun of himself gave him higher evaluations and expressed a greater likelihood of voting for him. The people who saw only the negative clip gave him lower evaluations and said they were less likely to vote for him.

Imagine that! It's the same topic (weight). The same person (Chris Christie). The same venue (David Letterman's show). The only change is that Christie brought it up himself. And that made all the difference.

Next, researchers looked at the power of self-deprecating humor in business. In this study, a professor at Seattle University had a senior business executive introduce a new employee named Pat to the group.[58] In the first instance, the executive said: "I am so glad that Pat took this job despite knowing all about *me*." In the second instance, he said, "I am so glad that Pat took this job despite knowing all about *you*." The third time, he said, "I am so glad that Pat took this job."

The leader who used self-deprecating humor ("I am so glad Pat took this job despite knowing all about *me*") was ranked as being more trustworthy, more likable, and having better leadership skills. It showed that self-deprecating humor can be a powerful tool for CEOs and executives because it minimizes the differences in status between the leaders and their employees. The leader who used negative humor toward his employees received a worse evaluation than the leader who used no humor at all.

And self-deprecating humor works in life. In 2010, Brené Brown, then a little-known college professor from Texas, gave a TEDx Talk called "The Power of Vulnerability." Brown's speech resonated with people and became one of the top five most-viewed TED Talks with more than 50 million views. Her message was that we connect with people by being vulnerable, authentic, and real. She said that vulnerability is a sign of courage, not weakness.

Brown delivered her famous talk by using lots of self-deprecating humor and showed her own vulnerability by candidly discussing her mental breakdown and subsequent visits with a therapist. That little talk gave Brown a platform to spread her insightful message, and she has since authored six number-one *New York Times* bestsellers.

Stumbling onto the Secret

I stumbled onto the power of self-deprecating humor. Shortly after graduating from law school, I met Jeb Bush. He was a young guy at the time and had never held elective office before. I wrote a joke for

Jeb's first campaign for governor, and the joke became the icebreaker for his stump speech. The line was: "One of my opponents accused me of running on my father's coattails. To show that I'm running on my own merits, I've decided to change my last name. I don't know what I'm going to change it to yet. But it's either going to be Reagan or Eisenhower." Jeb eventually got elected as governor.

During Jeb's first year in office, I filed my papers to run for the U.S. Congress. I was criticized during my first race for Congress for my lack of experience. My opponents each had eight years of experience—one as mayor, the other as a state legislator. I had zero years of experience as an elected official. During a campaign debate, one of them said I was an "amateur." I said, "Yes, I am an amateur. But it was amateurs who built Noah's Ark, and professionals who built the Titanic." I didn't hear about that issue anymore.

It was because of this same issue that I discovered Senator Bob Dole was very funny. Dole, who won the GOP nomination for president in 1996, was in Orlando to do a press conference for me in 2000, a few days before my first election. After Dole endorsed me, a member of the press asked Dole if I had enough political experience (zero) to serve in Congress. Dole replied, "I'd be president right now if I didn't have so much damn experience. Too many bad votes. Keller has just the right amount of experience. No bad votes at all."

Luckily, against all odds, I ended up winning. From the beginning, I wanted to do good by increasing Pell Grants, but I firmly believe it was self-deprecating humor that lifted me up to a position to be able to make it happen.

Once I got to Congress, I took my job, but not myself, seriously. For example, once I was asked to dedicate a new bus station in downtown Orlando for which I had obtained federal funding. However, instead of simply calling it a "bus station," it was called a "Regional Intermodal Center." Using big words unnecessarily is a pet peeve of mine. To make a point of how silly it was, I gave the following remarks at the ribbon-cutting ceremony:

"I am proud to be here at the unveiling of the Regional Intermodal Center. Or, as I like to call it, 'the RIC.' Before I was elected to Congress, I wasn't very sophisticated. I used to refer to a 'Regional Intermodal Center' as a 'bus station.' Now I know better. In fact, after I leave here today, I plan to take the 'Mass Transportation Delivery Vehicle,' or 'bus,' down the 'Multi-directional Hardened Surface Transportation Aid,' or 'road,' through several 'Electronic Traffic Control Devices,' or 'stop lights,' on my way to the 'Accelerated Nutritional Center,' or 'McDonald's.' At that time, as a 'Fitness-Challenged Public Servant,' or 'fat congressman,' I plan on ordering a 'Thermally Enhanced Fruit Pastry,' or 'hot apple pie.'"

Supremely Funny

I've seen Supreme Court justices effectively use self-deprecating humor. Justice Samuel Alito testified at a Judiciary Committee hearing when I was there. He wanted federal judges to get a pay raise. I got to question him. I said, "I hear you, but life isn't fair, is it? Judge Judy makes $28 million a year, but you only get paid $200,000."

Justice Alito replied, "My mother religiously watches Judge Judy almost every afternoon. And she thinks that Judge Judy does a much better job than we do and deserves more money."[59] The room erupted. We voted for the pay raise.

Another example was Justice Ruth Bader Ginsburg. The Notorious RBG had a funny habit of falling asleep at the State of the Union speeches. One time, the camera caught her totally asleep, head bent down. She could have faked it and said she was meditating or concentrating on the president's words. Instead, she was refreshingly candid. She said she "wasn't 100 percent sober" because she had a bit too much wine at dinner. Such a human, relatable response. Frankly, I wish I had a couple bottles of wine before those long-winded speeches, too.

The Queen's Speech

Nobody's too important to use self-deprecating humor. In May of 2007, President Bush welcomed Queen Elizabeth II to the White House and, while speaking on the South Lawn, made a verbal gaffe that added two hundred years to her age. "You dined with ten US presidents. You helped our nation celebrate its bicentennial in 1776 ... in 1976." He paused, winked at the queen, and then turned to the audience and said, "She gave me a look that only a mother could give a child."[60]

It didn't faze the queen a bit. She was a good sport. Later, at a formal dinner at the British ambassador's residence in Washington, the Queen opened her speech with a smile, saying, "I wondered whether I should start this toast by saying, 'When I was here in 1776 ... '" President Bush and the other guests burst out in laughter.[61]

The Mount Rushmore of Presidential Humor

Other presidents were also masters at using self-deprecating humor to deflect criticism. If there was a Mount Rushmore for humor, it would likely include Abraham Lincoln, Ronald Reagan, JFK, and Barack Obama.

During a debate, Abe Lincoln's opponent accused him of being "two-faced." Lincoln replied, "Two-faced? If I had another face, do you think I'd be wearing this one?" Of course, that face is now up on the real Mount Rushmore.

Ronald Reagan was in his mid-seventies when he ran for re-election. He seemed a bit confused and out of it during the first debate. During the second debate, the moderator asked Reagan if he was too old to be president. Reagan replied, "I will not make age an issue of this campaign. I am not going to exploit, for political purposes, my opponent's youth and inexperience." Everyone laughed, including his opponent, Walter Mondale. Mondale later said, "I knew at that moment my campaign was over." Reagan won forty-nine of fifty states—the biggest landslide in history. He used his second term to help end the Cold War.

On the Democrat side, John F. Kennedy had a great sense of humor. During his campaign against Nixon, JFK spoke at a dinner banquet. He pulled a piece of paper from his pocket and said, "I just received this wire from my generous daddy. 'Dear Jack, don't buy a single vote more than is necessary. I'll be damned if I'm going to pay for a landslide.'"

After winning, the first thing President Kennedy did was announce that he was appointing his younger brother Robert Kennedy as attorney general. It was a huge controversy. Bobby Kennedy was only thirty-five years old. He had never tried a single case in any federal or state court. And there was a nepotism problem. Even the *New York Times* came out against it.[62] What did JFK do? He deflected the issue with humor. He said, "I don't see anything wrong with giving Bobby a little legal experience before he goes out on his own to practice law."[63] A year later, we had the Cuban Missile Crisis. For thirteen days, our country was on the verge of a nuclear war with Russia. And it was Bobby Kennedy who helped negotiate the peaceful solution.

Barack Obama was also very good at using self-deprecating humor, especially at the White House Correspondents' Association dinners. He said, "I'm hard at work on plans for the Obama library. And some have suggested that we put it in my birthplace, but I'd rather keep it in the United States." He also joked about getting older. He said, "These days, I look in the mirror, and I have to admit, I'm not the strapping young Muslim socialist that I used to be." It was the next day after one of those White House Correspondents' dinners that Obama's most important decision was implemented. SEAL Team Six captured and killed Osama bin Laden.

If you look at the Mount Rushmore of funny presidents, you will see that all had something in common. All of them connected with people by being authentic, human, and by not taking themselves too seriously. All of them were able to get their jobs, in part, because of their great sense of humor. And all of them used their positions to do great things.

As a result, the slaves were freed, nuclear war was averted, the Cold War was brought to an end, and Osama bin Laden was brought to justice. A little humor can change your life . . . and maybe the world.

TAKEAWAY

Self-deprecating humor is a powerful tool in politics, business, and life. We connect with each other by being authentic, by being vulnerable, and by not taking ourselves too seriously. It takes courage and self-confidence to use self-deprecating humor, but if you can do it, something magical happens. You can relax people, lower walls, and build rapport. The best leaders are able to expertly use self-deprecating humor to deflect criticism, diffuse tense situations, and acknowledge flaws or mistakes.

The power of self-deprecating humor can be harnessed by anyone, including you. You don't have to be the president. You don't have to be a member of Congress. You don't have to be the funniest person in the room.

All you have to be is the most authentic version of yourself. What you thought were your biggest weaknesses are really your greatest strengths. They are the very things that help connect you with other people.

Don't fake it till you make it. Be real to seal the deal. If you can laugh at yourself and at life, you will be unstoppable.

CHAPTER 10
Networking the Right Way

"The single greatest 'people skill' is a highly developed and authentic interest in the other person."

—Bob Burg

Successful networking is all about developing relationships. It's not about trying to get something as fast as you can. This type of short-term strategy makes people feel used and never works over the long haul. Dorie Clark, a frequent contributor to *Harvard Business Review*, provides the best networking advice I've ever seen in her excellent book, *The Long Game: How to Be a Long-Term Thinker in a Short-Term World.*[64] This chapter will cover the three principles of success for networking advocated by Clark, and I will share three real-life stories to illustrate.

The Principles of Networking for Success

#1 Maintain authentic relationships with people you admire.

You should develop and maintain relationships with interesting people you admire and want to spend more time with.[65] If you connect authentically with quality people without an agenda and deepen your relationship over the long term, there are at least five possible outcomes:

1. They may be helpful to you down the road;
2. If they can't help you, based upon the "Six Degrees of Separation" principles, there is a good chance they may know someone who knows someone who can help you;
3. You never end up needing their help;
4. You end up being able to help them—knowingly or unknowingly, or;
5. There is nothing you can do to help each other, but you've spent time with people you wanted to hang out with anyway.

#2 No asks for a year.

Dorie Clark says, "Avoid asking new connections for any kind of meaningful favor for at least a year, to take the pressure off the relationship and to ensure they're clear that you're not making friends just to take advantage of them."[66] By that, Clark means not asking for favors that require them to spend political capital for a year. Example A: "Hey, so great to meet you last night at the cocktail reception. As I mentioned, I'd like to be a judge. I think I'd be a perfect fit. Since you know the governor, would you call him and ask him to appoint me judge?" Answer: NOT COOL. (And, yes, people do that. It makes you feel used.) Example B: "I'm new. Can you recommend a good dry cleaner/tailor/dentist?" Answer: COOL. (It requires no political capital, and it's an easy lift.)

Of course, it's appropriate to ask favors of your closest friends in dire moments when you truly need help, such as a job situation. Those are not new connections. As the saying goes, "A good friend will help you move. A great friend will help you move a body." I share a story later in the chapter about how one good friend ended up saving me. However, if it is a new connection, it should really be a true, time-dependent emergency before you ask for a favor. That certainly does occur, and I'll give an example of that type of situation as well.

#3 Bring value to the exchange.

The relationship should be reciprocal. Just because the other person is powerful, wealthy, or super successful in their field, don't assume you have nothing to offer. Be creative. You can contribute sweat equity. You can connect them with others. You can offer to help them in an area outside their sphere of power.[67] For example, as a young guy, I wrote a joke for Jeb Bush's campaign for governor. You might have weight-lifting or running advice that an executive could use. You may have tips about your city for someone who just moved here. You could volunteer to help a senior leader in your organization prepare her presentation for an upcoming meeting.

Sandra Day O'Connor: The Power of Friendship

We could all learn a lot from Supreme Court Justice Sandra Day O'Connor about the power of networking and maintaining friendships.

Brush with Greatness

I was in high school when Sandra Day O'Connor made the cover of *Time* magazine as the first female Supreme Court justice. A few years later, I read her Supreme Court opinions in law school. It never occurred to me that one day our paths would cross. But they did.

During my first year in Congress, I was a last-minute fill-in for another congressman who had an emergency. He was supposed to introduce Justice O'Connor to a group of high school students. I was happy to help. When I arrived at the Supreme Court, Justice O'Connor's assistant ushered me back to her private chambers. Justice O'Connor warmly greeted me and invited me to take a seat. She said, "Congressman, since you're going to be introducing me, I thought we'd get to know each other a little bit."

It was a surreal moment. After a little small talk, I said, "I've always wanted to know: what was it like for you getting that telephone call from President Reagan, telling you that you're going to be the first woman in history on the Supreme Court?"

Meeting Justice Sandra Day O'Connor before I had the honor of introducing her at an assembly.

She said, "I was quite surprised. My interview with President Reagan was only about fifteen minutes long. We talked about ranching and riding horses. It was small talk. He didn't ask me about any legal issues.

Afterward, I was in the airplane flying back to Arizona and thought to myself, *Well, I'm sure not getting that job.* A few days later, I was working in my office [Arizona state appellate court] when the telephone rang. The president was on the line. He said, 'Sandra, I'd like to announce your nomination to the US Supreme Court tomorrow. If that is all right with you?'" She said she accepted on the spot and flew to DC for the announcement.

When Bill Met Sandy

Sandra Day O'Connor went to law school with William "Bill" Rehnquist at Stanford. They sat next to each other, studied together, were moot court partners, and dated for a while. Rehnquist even popped the question in a letter to her. He said, "To be specific, Sandy, will you marry me this summer?" Evan Thomas wrote about the marriage proposal in his biography of Justice O'Connor, *First: Sandra Day O'Connor.*[68]

She declined the marriage proposal, but she treasured Rehnquist's friendship, and they remained close personal friends for thirty years. Rehnquist was appointed to the Supreme Court in 1972. In 1981, Ronald Reagan announced he would fulfill a campaign promise by appointing a woman to the Supreme Court. Her old law school buddy Rehnquist recommended O'Connor to Reagan. It made the difference. Reagan selected the little-known Arizona state court appellate judge on July 7, 1981.[69]

Young John

The next big hurdle was to navigate O'Connor through the treacherous waters of the Senate Judiciary hearings and the vote of the full Senate. She didn't have any federal experience. To help O'Connor get through it, the Justice Department assigned a young staffer named John to assist her. John was a bright young lawyer, fresh off a clerkship with Justice Rehnquist.

Together, John and O'Connor were a good team. It was the first televised confirmation hearing for a Supreme Court justice. She did well, and America fell in love with her. The Senate approved her nomination by a vote of 99–0. (The one senator who missed the vote said he would have voted for her, too.) Rehnquist and O'Connor would sit next to each other again—this time on the Supreme Court—for the next twenty-four years.

I lived right behind the Supreme Court in a small Capitol Hill apartment. On a few occasions, I passed Chief Justice Rehnquist on the sidewalk on my walk by the Court on the way to the Cannon House Office Building. He was always bundled up in a coat and wore a cabbie-style hat. I was surprised he didn't have security with him.

In September 2005, Chief Justice Rehnquist passed away. I was in my third term and was curious to see who President George W. Bush would pick. Bush was looking for someone who was young and smart to serve on the Court for a long time. Justice O'Connor knew, and recommended, someone who was young and smart—that guy John who had helped guide her through the Senate confirmation process.

Young John only had two years of experience as a judge at the time, but he was bright, capable, and well-connected. On September 24, 2005, young John—better known as John G. Roberts Jr.—was approved by the Senate and became the youngest chief justice of the United States Supreme Court in more than two hundred years.[70]

I would cross paths with Chief Justice Roberts not too long after. The Judiciary Committee was dealing with judicial compensation issues, and the chief justice was seeking more compensation for the federal district court trial judges. Mike Pence, who was on Judiciary with me, gave me a heads-up that the chief justice would be calling me.

The call came a couple days later. "Hi Congressman, this is John Roberts," he said humbly. No title. Not "Chief Justice Roberts" or "Justice Roberts," just "John Roberts." I thought to myself, *Man, this guy is good at relationships.*

Home by Thanksgiving

In August of 2006, I was the keynote speaker at a luncheon for the Central Florida Association for Women Lawyers in Orlando. Afterward, one of the attorneys, Liz McCausland, asked to speak with me privately.

"Will you help me?"

As the audience trickled out of the banquet room of the Citrus Club in downtown Orlando, Liz told me her mom had been locked up in a Vietnamese prison for a year. I asked her for details.

Me: "So, tell me about it."

Liz: "Where do I start?"

Me: "How about tell me a little about your mom."

Liz: "Her name is Cuc Foshee. She was born in Vietnam and is a US citizen. She owns a local commercial landscaping company. You've actually met her." (Liz showed me a picture of her mom, Thuong Nguyen "Cuc" Foshee, standing next to Vice President Dick Cheney and me at a luncheon.)

Me: "What happened?"

Liz: "It started a year ago on September 8, 2005. She had traveled to Vietnam to attend a nephew's wedding. As she was driving down the road, she was pulled over and arrested."

Me: "Arrested for what?"

Liz: "We didn't know at the time. We didn't even know where she was for a few weeks."

Me: "What was she charged with?"

Liz: "They still haven't charged her. No attorney, no due process, nothing."

Me: "And she's still in jail?"

Liz: "Yes, it's been a year. She's in a small jail cell in Ho Chi Minh City."

Me: "When is she getting out?"

Liz: "We have no idea. We don't know if she will ever be released or allowed to return to the United States."

Me: "Okay, so no formal charges. But what reason are they giving for keeping her locked up this long?"

Liz: "At some point, the Vietnamese government told her she was suspected of terrorist activity. They define terrorism broadly to mean anything that poses a threat to the government."

Me: "What did she do?"

Liz: "She is active in Orlando's Vietnamese American community and speaks in favor of democracy in Vietnam. Prior to her arrival in Vietnam, she had given interviews to a local Orlando radio station, saying that people should be allowed to elect their leaders. She attended a pro-democracy rally and met with the leader of a group who advocates for democratic elections in Vietnam."

Me: "All of this on American soil?"

Liz: "Yes."

Me: "Crazy."

Liz: *"Will you help me?"*

Me: "Yes, I'll help you."

Liz: "Thank you."

Me: *"We'll have your mom home by Thanksgiving."* (I wasn't sure why, but my instinct told me to tell her that.)

Leverage

Liz was a prominent lawyer with lots of contacts. Over the past year, she had already tried nearly everything. For example, the law firm of Holland & Knight was kind enough to offer their services pro bono, and the US consul also tried to intervene. Still, they were not able to secure her freedom.

I looked into it. We needed political leverage. And we had it.

It was lucky timing. There was a bill pending in Congress that would be worth over $10 *billion* in terms of Vietnam's trade exports to the United States. The legislation—to grant Vietnam Permanent Normalized Trade Relations (PNTR) status—was hugely important to Vietnam's government because they needed PNTR status to become a member of the World Trade Organization (WTO) and increase their exports.

The PNTR bill was expected to have plenty of support in the Senate (free-trade friendly), but it was in trouble in the House and needed a few votes to pass. The date of the vote had not yet been set, but it was expected to take place later in 2006.

The other political leverage we had was that President George W. Bush was expected to attend an economic summit in Vietnam in mid-November 2006. If the PNTR bill were still not approved by Congress by then, the Vietnamese government would have extra incentive to be cooperative.

Therefore, the secret to securing Cuc Foshee's release was to block the vote by the House and Senate on PNTR until she was safely home in Florida.

Team Effort

Senator Mel Martinez (R-FL) was a great partner every step of the way. And we had a good game plan.

On my end, I requested the House leadership to delay the vote on PNTR. I got the personal cell phone of Vietnam's ambassador in Washington (Chien Nguyen) from our US ambassador to Vietnam (Michael W. Marine). I then called Ambassador Nguyen and bluntly explained that Vietnam would not get PNTR status unless my constituent were set free.

On his end, Senator Martinez threatened to hold up the bill in the Senate and spoke directly with President George W. Bush and Secretary of State Condoleezza Rice about the situation while flying on Air Force One.

The behind-the-scenes drama unfolded as planned and drew media attention. For example, on October 29, 2006, the *Orlando Sentinel* reported:

> "The 58-year-old Foshee's plight could derail negotiations to open trade between the United States and Vietnam. US Sen. Mel Martinez, R-FL, has vowed to block Congress's mid-November vote to solidify permanent trade with the Asian country—a fast-growing market for US goods—until Foshee is released. . . . Martinez brought Foshee's case directly to Secretary of State Condoleezza Rice and President Bush, who is scheduled to attend the Asia-Pacific Economic Cooperation Summit in Vietnam in November."[71]

"Keller spent time on the phone with ambassadors and lawmakers, urging the Vietnamese government to release Thuong Nguyen 'Cuc' Foshee, a Vietnamese-born Orlando woman imprisoned for her pro-democracy views. He politely played hardball with Chien Nguyen, the Vietnamese ambassador in Washington, telling him that he has the votes to halt an upcoming free-trade bill with Vietnam. While the ambassador tried to argue, Keller cut him short. 'She's been in prison thirteen months; that's enough,' he said."[72]

"You Look Sick"

The Vietnamese government was in a pinch. It was November 10, 2006. The final vote on PNTR had been delayed, and President George W. Bush would be arriving on November 17, 2006, for his first-ever visit to Vietnam to attend the Asia-Pacific Economic Cooperation Summit.

To save face, they quickly held a sham, one-day "trial." They "convicted" Foshee of terrorism, which was nebulously defined to mean any action that opposes or threatens the government (including Foshee's radio interview supporting democracy). The Vietnamese court sentenced Cuc Foshee to fifteen months in jail, with credit for "time served." That meant that Cuc would still have to serve another month in jail and would not be home until mid-December.

That was unacceptable. We let Vietnam know that the PNTR bill would be blocked until Foshee was safely home.

Once again, Vietnam found a way to save face. Within hours of hearing our objections, a jail guard appeared at Foshee's cell.

Guard: "You look sick."

Cuc: "I'm not sick."

Guard: "Yes, we think you look sick. *We're sending you home to America*."[73]

She was immediately set free. The nightmare was over. On November 12, 2006, Cuc Foshee arrived on American soil.

Happy Thanksgiving

Cuc Foshee's daughter and younger sister were there to meet her at San Francisco's airport on November 12, 2006. After spending a week recuperating in California, Foshee boarded a flight back to Orlando.

On November 20, 2006, Senator Martinez and I celebrated with Cuc Foshee and her family at an emotional homecoming party in Orlando. We both gave Cuc big hugs. "Funny, you don't look like a terrorist," Martinez joked to our diminutive, five-foot-one constituent, who wore a pretty black dress and a grateful smile. Cuc posed for a photograph with Senator Martinez and me.

As we took the picture, I thought back to my first conversation with Cuc's daughter, Liz, after my luncheon speech to the women lawyers' group in August 2006.

For some reason, unknown to me, my instinct had told me back then to reassure Liz that her mom would be safely home in Orlando before Thanksgiving. It was three days before Thanksgiving.

Trade Bill Aftermath

After Cuc Foshee was safely home, I received a call from Vietnam's Ambassador Nguyen—the same person I'd dealt with in seeking her release.

Ambassador: "Are you very happy?"

Me: "Yes."

Ambassador: "Do you remember?"

Me: "Yes, I remember. I said I would support PNTR only if Cuc Foshee is released."

Ambassador: "Will you honor?"

Me: "Yes, I will honor it." (It was not a tough vote for me. I've always felt that trade with low tariffs was good for both countries.)

In early December 2006, Congress voted in favor of granting PNTR status to Vietnam. In his speech on the Senate floor in favor of PNTR, Senator Martinez honored Cuc Foshee and said:

"We recently celebrated, in Orlando, her return home. Congressman Ric Keller was also there, my colleague, who step-by-step was a partner for me in seeking the release of Mrs. Foshee. . . . I will never do anything greater than to have played a part in securing the freedom of one individual."[74]

In mid-December 2006, President Bush signed the PNTR bill into law. In early January 2007, Vietnam was granted admission into the WTO, and their 2007 exports to the US exceeded $10 billion for the first time.

I joked to Cuc Foshee's daughter, Liz, "Did it go to your mom's head that she is worth over $10 billion?" She laughed and said, "Yes! Every day!" (They're both actually very humble.)

The Text

As I write these words, it's been sixteen years since Cuc Foshee was freed. Every November 12, I wake up to the sound of a "ding" on my cell phone. It's always a text from Liz. It says: "Thank you. This is the day you saved my mom's life."

What Liz doesn't fully appreciate is that *she* is the one who saved her mom's life. Her aggressive networking—reaching out to everyone she knew, connecting to those she didn't know, attending events so she could meet others beyond her network, and humbly and gratefully asking everyone for help—is what saved her mom.

Furthermore, Liz is a generous and kind person who had been building authentic, selfless relationships her entire life. In her time of need, people were more than happy to help her or introduce her to people who could.

Important relationships don't just fall into your lap; you have to seek them out and make them happen. If she had sat at home, waiting for the right person to find out about her dilemma, or for the Vietnamese government to change its mind, or if she didn't already have a vast network of people she had helped through the years (who were now willing to help her), the outcome may have been different.

Cuc Foshee, her daughter Liz, and me at Liz's birthday party in 2022.

Help Wanted

The November 2008 wave election swept me out of office. I had a family to support and only two months to find a job. Nobody wanted me. Not in Washington, DC, and not in Orlando.

Why? It was simple. In DC, after the 2008 elections, the U.S. House, Senate, and White House were firmly controlled by Democrats. As a result, the DC trade associations and lobbying firms were laying off Republicans and hiring well-connected Democrats.

The idea of being a lobbyist didn't appeal to me anyway, but I thought I would have made a good CEO of a trade association for an industry within my specialty areas, such as the Motion Picture Association, recording industry, higher education, or tourism/travel. But there were zero options at the time.

In Orlando, because of the recession, the large law firms (especially those that did real estate) were shrinking in size. The big firms, some of whom were laying off 20 percent of their attorneys, were not in a position to take on any new, big salary.

To no avail, I spent hours on the phone every day, calling my contacts. People need you when they need you. Some people who pretended to be "good friends" and "loyal supporters" when I was in Congress were no longer taking my calls or agreeing to meet with me.

It was like the David Spade skit on *SNL* where he played a receptionist for Dick Clark Productions. The receptionist would block visitors by using condescending questions:

"And you are?"

"And he would know you from?"

"And it is regarding?"

"And did you have an appointment?"

Humorously, in the *SNL* skit, even Jesus and Roseanne Barr were blocked by the gatekeeping secretary. That skit was how my life went the first two months after Congress.

Lucky Break

And then I caught a lucky break on the job front.

Before serving in Congress, I had been a partner at a large law firm called Rumberger, Kirk, & Caldwell. I had not practiced law in eight years but luckily had kept my law license active.

Three of my Rumberger colleagues (Chris Hill, Ken Rugh, and Steve Main) had split off from Rumberger and started their own civil litigation law firm. They had about twenty-five employees, and the firm was growing. I had lunch with my old buddy Chris Hill and told him the truth.

It was like another scene from the *Seinfeld* episode called "The Opposite," where George Costanza does just the opposite of what normal people would do.

"Chris, here's my sales pitch. I'm screwed. Nobody wants me. Not in DC, not in Orlando. I have not practiced law in eight years. Could you guys give me a job?" Luckily, they said yes. It was very gracious of them. I had no clients at the time. I eventually became an equity partner at the law firm of Hill, Rugh, Keller, & Main; made more money; and married the love of my life.

It was a long-term, authentic relationship with Chris, someone I liked and admired, that saved me. The same thing will save you.

TAKEAWAY

The guiding principles for great networking are authenticity, reciprocity, and being in it for the long haul. The caricature of bad networking is using people and trying to get something as fast as you can. The three key rules to remember are: (1) develop and maintain authentic relationships with interesting people you admire, (2) no asks for a year, and (3) bring value to the relationship.

CHAPTER 11
Mentors and Sponsors

"Show me a successful individual, and I'll show you someone who had real positive influences in his life. I don't care what you do for a living—if you do it well, I'm sure there was someone cheering you on or showing you the way. A mentor."

—Denzel Washington

I have been a fan of mentoring programs since I was in fourth grade. By that time, my mom had gone through her second divorce. She was raising three kids—my younger sister, brother, and me—alone on the modest salary of a secretary.

I wouldn't meet my biological father until I was fourteen. My stepfather didn't keep in touch with me or his two biological children after they split up. My mom, who never married again, wanted me to have a positive male role model in my life. She signed me up for the Big Brothers Big Sisters mentoring program.

I was matched up with a kind man named Tom Luke, who worked for the *Orlando Sentinel*. He looked like Burt Reynolds and drove a gold-colored sports car. For several years, Tom would pick me up every Tuesday afternoon at my elementary school. We would go to dinner, play catch with the football, or go to events like his company picnic. I surprised my mom when I came home with a new tennis racket that I won in the company dodgeball contest. I always looked forward to those Tuesdays, and I was grateful for his investment in time to make sure I turned out okay.

Florida Mentoring

Mentoring had been a great experience for me as a kid, and I wanted to pay it forward. When I graduated from law school, I heard about the Orlando/Orange County COMPACT program. It was a mentoring program for students at risk of dropping out of high school. At the time, Florida had a graduation rate of only 53 percent, the worst in the nation, but 98 percent of the kids in the COMPACT program stayed in school.

I signed up to be a mentor for a student at my alma mater, Boone High School. After the student graduated, I mentored a second student until he also graduated. I was invited to serve on the COMPACT board of directors. I learned that there were about 700 students in Orange County who still needed to be matched with mentors. I made it my mission to recruit new mentors. I gave about fifty speeches to various Rotary clubs, chambers of commerce, and bar associations throughout the community and was able to recruit 700 new mentors.

I was then elected chairman of the COMPACT board of directors, and we maintained the 98 percent success rate of kids staying in school.

Nebraska Mentoring

Meanwhile, as I'm doing the COMPACT program, a new mentoring program called TeamMates was started in Lincoln, Nebraska. Tom Osborne, the head coach of the University of Nebraska football team, and his wife, Nancy, started the mentoring program to help middle school students stay in school and reach their potential. The program began in 1991 when Coach Osborne recruited twenty-five volunteers from his football team to be matched with twenty-five boys from area middle schools.[75] TeamMates was successful and expanded statewide. "I truly believe that my mom and dad's legacy will be the statewide mentoring program that they started years ago," said Suzanne Hince, Tom and Nancy Osborne's youngest daughter.[76] That is pretty high praise for a man who won three national championships at Nebraska.

Joining Forces

Albert Einstein said, "Coincidence is God's way of remaining anonymous." I have come to believe that so-called "coincidences" are often meaningful events. We are all connected. I don't think it's purely a random accident that the right people and events come into our lives at just the right time.

Consider the events and "coincidences" that came together at the perfect moment in time for Coach Osborne and me to join forces and pass legislation that helped provide up to 200,000 mentors nationwide. The common denominators of Tom Osborne and me:

1. We both led successful mentoring programs in our communities in the 1990s.

2. We were both elected to Congress on the same day, November 7, 2000.

3. We sat next to each other on the House Education Committee for six years.

4. We co-chaired the Mentoring Caucus.

5. We co-sponsored a resolution approved by the US House of Representatives, encouraging mentoring programs.

6. We coauthored legislation called the Mentoring for Success Act, which passed Congress and was signed into law by President George W. Bush as part of his education reform legislation.

Finding a Mentor

The bottom line is that mentoring is important on both sides of the equation. It's good to have one and to be one. Here are five tips on seeking a mentor in connection with your goals or business.

1. Seek out a mentor who is already doing what you want to do. If you're opening a flower shop, talk to other people who successfully run flower shops in other communities.

2. Ask people about how they built their business or accomplished their goals. Most people love to talk about this and will be happy to share their advice.

3. When speaking with your mentor or prospective mentor, be efficient with their time and make it brief, especially in your first conversation.

4. Write down in advance the specific questions or points you'd like to cover in your initial conversation.

5. Asking for advice is great, but do NOT ask for any favors within the first year that require them to expend their political capital, unless it is truly an emergency.

Some might say, "Well, why not ask them for favors? I need to succeed as soon as possible. Besides, it doesn't hurt to ask, right?" *Wrong.* In this context, it does hurt to ask. Here are the dos and don'ts. DO be brief, authentic, well-prepared, and grateful for the advice. DO NOT ask them to expend political capital on behalf of a stranger or new acquaintance, and don't come into the meeting with a preconceived agenda for them to help you ASAP. Why? People don't like feeling used. The more you follow the DOs, the more likely they will be to return your e-mails, meet with you again, and help you in the future.

The Difference Between a Mentor and a Sponsor

As already discussed, mentorship is extraordinarily important. However, an extremely important relationship that is not discussed or understood enough is sponsorship. Think of sponsorship as mentorship on steroids. Sponsors are similar to mentors in that they also provide critical advice, coaching, and direction, but sponsors differ from mentors in that they are individuals who are willing to advocate for you, fight for you, and risk their political capital for your success.

In other words, mentors provide advice and feedback. Sponsors use their influence and power to advocate on your behalf to make partner, get a promotion, or raise your pay. This also includes endorsing you for public office over other candidates, nominating you for visible committees or projects within your company, writing your business school recommendation letters, sharing how things *really* work in your company behind the scenes, or standing by you and your position in a heated debate with another department. They have senior decision-making authority within your company, firm, school, or office, and have a seat at the table when important decisions are made.

I'll give you the best example I've ever seen. It happened at a partners' meeting when I was with a big Orlando law firm. (To protect privacy, names have been changed, along with non-essential details.) "Betty" was a senior associate up for partner. She had been passed over for partner for two years in a row. Many in the room thought Betty was a nice enough person but merely an average lawyer and not a great candidate for partner.

But this year was different from the last two years in one major respect. This time, Betty had a sponsor, and not just any sponsor. "Adam" was a very powerful senior partner. He was well-liked and respected by the other partners. He had also been incredibly good to me back when I was an associate. When I was a young lawyer, Adam was the one who gave me trial experience. We did three trials in a row and won them all. In each case, he let me take the lead as the "first chair," which allowed me to do all of the fun and important parts, like the opening statement, cross-examining the key witnesses and parties, closing arguments, etc., while he took a back seat role as "second chair." Over the years, Adam had done something similar to help every person in that room.

Adam did two things. First, he said to the group something like: "I realize you guys don't think that she is a top-notch lawyer. But she handles most of the work for one of my big clients, and the client just loves her, and that's pretty important. I don't ask you guys for anything, but I want you with me on this one vote." Second, he didn't say, "Ric, I did that for you, so you need to do this for me." It was unneeded. It was simply something like, "This one thing is important to me. I would really appreciate a yes on this one." In other words, he was willing to cash in his chips to help this person make partner.

What happened? I voted yes and so did most of the other partners. She was approved with about 75 percent of the votes and only needed 50 percent. Without Adam as her sponsor, my educated guess is she would have got only about 20 percent of the vote. We weren't really voting for Betty. We were voting for Adam. Such is the power of a sponsor.

Hard Work Isn't Enough

Sponsorship is not talked about enough. We are told, or we assume, that if we work hard enough, we will be noticed and valued enough to earn the promotion, be selected for the coveted transfer, win the nomination, receive the honor, or achieve whatever goal is set out for us. That is not solely the case. In addition to excellent performance, we need people advocating for us along the way. Promotions aren't always determined by your work product: In a situation where all candidates are top performers but there is only one senior position, sponsorship is often the final factor that lands the candidate the promotion. Candidates need someone willing to stick his or her neck out for them, saying their performance stands out above others, and putting their political capital on the line to say their candidate—of all qualified candidates—is truly the person for the job. Sadly, many don't recognize this until they've been overlooked for a role they felt they deserved.

We overemphasize skills and abilities and reputation without adequately recognizing the importance of personal relationships. There are numerous examples of people who have benefited from sponsorships (intentionally and not), while others—who did not fully understand the sponsorship concept—did not achieve specific career goals.

For example, the former minister of finance for an African country once told a story of an important role her team was trying to fill. They had narrowed the selection down to two candidates: one candidate was known as the hard worker, staying to finish assignments late in the evening and sometimes coming in on weekends. She was extremely dependable, and her work was always high quality. The other candidate was not the star performer but a good performer. She left work on time and would always be at happy hours and other social events with her colleagues.

Going into the meeting to finalize the selection, the minister thought Candidate One was the obvious choice and didn't expect much debate. However, the selection committee had more confidence in Candidate Two because they had built personal relationships with her and saw her as a visionary, a potential leader, and someone who could work well with people and build relationships necessary in a leadership role. Candidate One was definitely seen as a hard worker, but some questioned why she was working so hard: "Is she slow? Is she having problems getting her work done? Does she have the right people skills? We never see her away from her desk."

Ultimately, Candidate Two was given the role. Candidate Two clearly had sponsors sitting at the table, whereas Candidate One did not. If I was Candidate One's mentor, I would advise her to spend less time at her desk and focus more on building authentic relationships with a broader group of people so she can be seen as a potential leader within the ministry, rather than as the worker bee.

The Sponsorship Advantage in Business

Carice Anderson, author of *Intelligence Isn't Enough*, extensively describes the sponsorship and mentorship dynamic in the business world.[77] "A sponsor is someone who works in your company who does not just have a senior title but has influence, decision-making power, and a seat at the table when decisions [are being made] about promotions, developmental assignments, performance ratings, and bonuses."[78]

Anderson describes the differences between mentorship and sponsorship. Mentors are usually very experienced individuals inside or outside the organization who can provide advice about career, industry, work-life balance, functional expertise, and specific topics. It is not performance-based: strong and less-strong performers can have and benefit from mentor relationships. In fact, in some companies, weaker employees are offered extra mentorship for additional guidance to help improve performance. Mentors can usually have several mentees, and vice versa; mentees can have several mentors based on different needs. The relationship is cultivated over time, typically through one-on-one interactions. Many companies have formal mentorship programs in addition to informal mentoring relationships that happen organically.[79]

On the other hand, sponsors are not as common. Not everyone has a sponsor, and usually, one can't simply ask someone to be their sponsor. Given that sponsorship requires a willingness to put one's reputation on the line to support an individual, the sponsor has to believe in the person's abilities, talents, and long-term potential. This is not a decision made lightly and is usually determined over time after witnessing the individual's contributions to the organization. It requires significant, sustained top performance, as well as additional work outside the person's stated role, interpersonal skills, long-term potential in the organization, and culture fit.

Anderson states, "If I were to choose between having a mentor and having a sponsor, I would choose a sponsor."[80]

Sponsors and Mentors in Public Life

In the political sphere, a mentor would be an elected official giving campaign advice to a potential candidate, whereas a sponsor would be that same elected official publicly endorsing the candidate, introducing the candidate to his or her political network, and raising funds for the candidate.

Once again, I'll give you a real-life example. When I ran for Congress the first time, I had a mentor and a sponsor. My mentor was former Rep. Jimmy Quillen (R-TN). He gave me advice. My sponsor was former Rep. Joe Scarborough (R-FL), now the host of *Morning Joe* on MSNBC. He risked his political capital and went all in to help pull me across the finish line and win the race.

Here's the practical difference. In the early part of my campaign, I called Quillen for advice. He represented my hometown of Johnson City, Tennessee, in Congress for three decades. Also, I was in a crowded primary, and he had won his seat after a five-way GOP primary, so I was curious to hear how he did it. This was our telephone conversation:

Me: "Congressman Quillen, I am Ric Keller. I was born in Johnson City, graduated from ETSU, and I am running for an open seat for Congress down in Orlando. I hope to help people just like you did. I need some advice."

Quillen: "Win."

Me: "What?"

Quillen: "Win. Son, you can't do anything to help people unless you win. Win, then call me back."

Me: "Of course, but how do I win?"

Quillen: "Tell me about your race."

Me: "There are four candidates in the Republican primary. After that, a general election against the mayor, who is a Democrat. She's the favorite."

Quillen: "There is no general election unless you win the primary, right?"

Me: "Right."

Quillen: "Forget the general election for now. Just focus on winning over the primary voters."

Me: "Got it. Focus on winning over Republican primary voters. Tips?"

Quillen: "When there's such a crowded Republican primary, voters will be lucky to remember only one thing about each candidate."

Me: "Okay, one thing."

Quillen: "Make sure you know what your one thing is. Make sure the voters know what your one thing is. And raise enough money to have TV commercials and mail to drive home the message on that one thing. Good luck, son."

I really appreciated his advice. It helped me refocus my energies. It took twenty minutes.

Now, contrast that with Congressman Joe Scarborough, the story I described in Chapter 5. He, too, gave me advice. But he also publicly endorsed me. He donated $1,000 to my campaign. He flew down to Orlando from the Panhandle and did three campaign events for me. He sent his top-notch political director (Derek Kitts) to live in Orlando and work his butt off for my campaign for a whole month. In short, he went out on a limb for me and helped me. It meant a lot to me because I was the underdog, and very few people back then would stick their necks out for me. Mentors give advice. Sponsors stick their necks out for you—and the right people listen to what they have to say.

Executives Need Sponsors Too

Sponsorship isn't just for those early in their careers; it is critical at all points in your career. A senior executive at a professional services firm shared a story of how sponsorship saved her from a potentially damaging situation with the chairman of the board of her company. The executive was working on priorities set by the CEO (with whom she had worked for several years) while the board chair gave her negative feedback because he felt she should be working on *his* set of priorities. She reported directly to the CEO, so she immediately asked the CEO which priorities she should be working on and how to manage the board chair's disparaging comments. The CEO immediately told the board chair that he had no authority over the CEO's direct reports, that the direct reports followed the CEO's direction (which had already been approved by the board), and if the board had any issues with any of the executive team, they had to go through the CEO first. This is clearly an example of a sponsor going out on a limb and risking political capital for a subordinate! Not only did the CEO advocate and fight for the executive, but the CEO also increased the executive's salary. And in the next round of board elections, a new chair was elected.

Other Types of Sponsors

The mentor-sponsor dynamic plays out in many situations beyond business and politics. In applying for graduate schools, a mentor is someone who may tell you about the program they attended and give you advice on your application. A sponsor is someone who would additionally review and edit your application essays, write a stellar letter of recommendation, and call admissions to try to give you a leg up in the admissions process.

It's the manager at a grocery store who takes a liking to a motivated cashier and mentors and eventually sponsors her to become department manager and then general manager. It's the high school basketball coach who becomes a father figure to a few boys on his team, helping them on and off the court, inviting them to dinners at his home, guiding them to part-time jobs, or even shepherding them to college scholarships.

Seeking and Sustaining Sponsorship

Strive to build authentic relationships, do your best work, and you will find mentors and sponsors. Spend one less hour at your desk and one more hour connecting with others. If your company, organization, or school offers formal mentorship programs, sign up to participate. These relationships are much more important than you realize.

Sponsors don't always have to be the most senior members of the firm; they can be individuals with influence. If you are trying to get on a specific project, the project manager could be the person with the influence. If you are hoping to build your reputation as a strong writer, the person who manages your company's internal newsletter, or the PR lead who coordinates submissions to outside publications, would be considered sponsors, if they can support you in getting published.

Sponsorship becomes challenging when one moves cities, companies, or offices, which happens more frequently these days. Sponsorship is contingent on you understanding the key players in your company, office, division, function, or community, which takes time. More importantly, you have to build your reputation and social capital with key leaders, which is also not an overnight task. You need to show strong, consistent performance in the job you were hired to do, as well as make contributions in other areas of the company, likely taking on extra projects, providing training or coaching, or volunteering for other work that builds your personal brand.

It could take a few years to build a sponsorship relationship with an individual. If you are job-hopping every two years, your chances of building sustainable sponsorship relationships that both parties can benefit from are lower. Sponsors will often prioritize longer-term relationships with outstanding contributors they trust, over newer relationships with equally strong individuals.

The key is to recognize that sponsorships aren't transferable. If you find yourself in a situation where you are transferring to a new office, function, country, or division in the same company, try to establish relationships in advance of the move or have your current sponsors advocate and support building relationships with leadership in your new office. At the very least, recognize you will need to start from scratch, and carve out time to build those relationships with new potential sponsors. Similarly, try to cultivate sponsorship relationships with more than one person in case your sponsor retires or changes companies or roles.

Being a Mentor and Sponsor

Referring back to Denzel Washington's quote at the beginning of the chapter, you have likely benefited from mentorship and sponsorship throughout your education, career, and life, whether or not you realized it at the time. Reflect on your life: identify your mentors and sponsors, what roles they played, what lessons they taught you, and what you were able to achieve because of their influence.

Now think about how you can play similar roles for others. Don't keep the lessons to yourself but share them. Become a mentor and sponsor so you can help others achieve their big dreams as well.

TAKEAWAY

Hard work, intelligence, and talent are not enough. Spend one hour less at your desk and one hour more cultivating authentic personal relationships with mentors and sponsors. Mentors give advice. Sponsors advocate for you and risk their political capital for your success.

CHAPTER 12
Bold, Authentic Leadership

"When in doubt, tell the truth."

—Mark Twain

Bold leaders connect with people by having the courage to be authentic, truthful, and vulnerable. To be sure, on a short-term basis, the truth can be inconvenient or embarrassing. However, over the long term, being authentic—even when it is temporarily unpopular—enhances your credibility, earns you the respect of others, and connects you in a meaningful way. Speak your truth, but still be as diplomatic as possible to maintain the self-esteem of others.

The Big Secret

The world's best comedians, television talk show hosts, and TED Talk speakers know a secret about connecting with people. I stumbled onto the secret purely by accident. I lived in New York for a year in between college and law school. As a comedy fan, I spent my free time hanging out at the Catch a Rising Star comedy club in Manhattan.

I got to see the country's best comedians perform night after night. After a few months, I noticed a pattern. The comedians who really connected with the audience—and got the biggest laughs—had something in common. They were all authentic, truthful, and vulnerable.

The best comedians, TV hosts, and speakers know that the secret to connecting with others is having the courage to be authentic and truthful. Steve Harvey, one of the Kings of Comedy with the highest-grossing comedy tour in history, credits finally getting up the courage to be truthful and authentic (including jokes about divorces, setbacks, and mistakes) as the secret to his career taking off.[81]

In his book *Act Like a Success, Think Like a Success,* Harvey said, "What made Richard Pryor so great was his openness. Once I was no longer afraid to open up about me and my truth, things changed for me professionally. I think that's what makes me effective as a person of integrity on the radio or as a spokesman is that people know I am going to tell them the truth no matter what the truth is. You don't always have to agree with it, but I'm telling you my truth."[82]

Larry King: Nobody Connected Better

Larry King was the Emmy Award-winning television host of CNN's *The Larry King Show* for fifteen years. King got his start in radio broadcasting. The industry publication *Talkers Magazine* named King as the number-one television talk show host of all time and the fourth-greatest radio talk show of all time.[83] Nobody connected better. What was the secret to his success in broadcasting?

King told the story in a commencement address at the University of San Diego.[84] Ever since he was a kid, his dream was to be a radio broadcaster. He found a small station in Miami, Florida, that was willing to give him a job sweeping up the floors. Larry watched and learned from the other disc jockeys and patiently waited for his chance to break into the business.

On a Friday, the general manager of the radio station told King that a disc jockey who worked the morning shift had just quit. The GM told Larry he was giving him a shot to be on-air the following Monday morning. Excited, he practiced saying his name and opening lines all weekend.

He reported for work Monday morning. A few minutes before going on the air, the GM told him that Larry's real last name of Zeiger wouldn't be a good radio name. That morning, there was an ad in the *Miami Herald* newspaper for Kings Wholesale Liquors. The GM saw it and said, "How about Larry King?" That became his name from that moment on; he legally changed it two years later.

A few minutes later, it was 9:00 A.M., time to start the show, and King took his seat inside the control room and pushed the button to play the radio show's theme song. As the theme song faded, King turned up the microphone and got ready to speak. But when he opened his mouth, no words came out. He panicked and hit the button to play the theme song a second time.

He said to himself, *Well, I tried, but I can't do it. I don't have the guts. I thought I had it, but maybe I just wasn't cut out for radio. I'm too scared.*

Then the GM kicked open the door to the control room and yelled, "Larry, this is a communications business, dammit! Communicate!" and then slammed the door.[85] Then Larry did something that he would do for the rest of his life: tell the truth and be 100 percent real.

As the theme song faded, he turned on the microphone and said, "Ladies and gentlemen, good morning. This is my first day on the radio. My name is Larry King. And that's the first time I've ever said that. I've been sitting here scared to death, and you've been hearing music going up and down and probably wondering if there's an earthquake in the station. But I want to tell you I was scared to death. Because all my life I wanted to be in radio, and now I had my chance, and I was scared. So bear with me. I really want this to work, so now I'm going to do my best."[86]

As King told the graduating class, "At that minute, I had them. I was never nervous on radio or television again because I learned that day if you're honest with your audience, you can't go wrong."[87]

Brené Brown authored six number-one *New York Times* bestsellers, and her TED Talk has more than 50 million views. As I mentioned in Chapter 9, Brown has a simple message based on her decades of research and countless interviews: we connect with people by being vulnerable, authentic, and real, and the willingness to be vulnerable is a sign of courage, not weakness.

Netflix: An Unconventional Strategy for Success

Netflix is a film and television streaming service and production company. The bizarre true-crime documentary *Tiger King* was the most-viewed Netflix series of 2020 with 64 million viewers. Launched in 1997, Netflix grew to become one of the most innovative and successful companies in the world with more than 12,000 employees, 220 million customers, and annual revenues of $30 billion.[88]

What is their secret? One reason for their success is that Reed Hastings, the co-founder and CEO of Netflix, used an unconventional and courageous strategy. Reed created a culture where admitting mistakes and showing vulnerability were welcomed in order to build trust, learn from failure, and encourage innovative practices.

In their book *No Rules Rules: Netflix and the Culture of Reinvention,* Hastings and international business school INSEAD professor Erin Meyer share many stories about Netflix's culture of admitting mistakes, being authentic, and showing vulnerability.[89] All leaders and employees, including the CEO, frequently share their flaws and failures, which they call "sunshining." They have large, open feedback sessions with each other in addition to formal and informal one-on-one discussions. They want everyone to see that mistakes and failures are necessary and normal. They have seen that sharing mistakes builds trust, fosters forgiveness, facilitates learning, and promotes courage, leading to faster and more successful innovation.

This culture grew organically due, in part, to experiences earlier in Hastings' career. Prior to Netflix, he was the co-founder and CEO of Pure Software. His engineering background and lack of managerial experience led him to make several leadership and people-management mistakes, including the hiring and firing of five sales managers in five years. These blunders weighed heavily on him, so he went to the board, shared his mistakes, and offered his resignation. Several surprising things happened:

1. He felt immense relief upon "coming clean" and sharing these errors.

2. The board did not accept his resignation; in fact, they believed in him and his leadership more because he had been so honest and open.

3. This gave Hastings the courage to share the same information in his next all-employee meeting, explaining his mistakes and expressing regret for how he hurt the company.

4. This, in turn, led to greater trust and relief among his staff, who started sharing mistakes they had made that they had previously hidden.

5. This resulted in better relationships and more transparency across the company, giving Hastings better information to make decisions and manage the business.

After selling Pure Software, Hastings took these lessons when he co-founded Netflix. One of the most memorable examples of admitting and learning from failure is the short-lived, failed Qwikster, considered "the biggest mistake in Netflix history."[90]

Expecting the DVD mail business to decline in favor of streaming, Netflix split its streaming services from its DVD business; DVDs would be managed by a new company called Qwikster. This was accompanied by a price increase and more customer complexity, as subscribers now had to manage two web interfaces when previously, they could use one website for both their streaming and DVD needs.

Customers revolted. Netflix lost millions of subscribers, and stock value declined more than 75 percent. Hastings quickly apologized to customers and took responsibility within the company. He also used this opportunity to figure out what went wrong, especially when they had been striving to build a culture of open feedback and transparency. He learned that many people thought the idea was bad from the outset but were afraid to vocalize disagreement, especially to him as CEO. This failure led to adjustments in culture and expectations: now the company insists on prioritizing the company's well-being over pleasing the boss, insomuch as stating that an employee is being disloyal to Netflix if that person doesn't share a dissenting opinion.[91]

Needless to say, Netflix rebounded from that mistake, learned as an organization, and continues to value and benefit from transparency, authenticity, and humility.

John McCain: The Straight Talk Express

Senator John McCain, the war hero and former GOP nominee for president, had a reputation as a straight-talking maverick who spoke his truth no matter what. I learned that firsthand. It was November 6, 2000, the day before my election, and Senator McCain had traveled all the way to Orlando to help me. McCain's message of "straight talk" appealed to moderate voters and independents, and the goal was for McCain to attract lots of press and hopefully push me over the top in this fifty-fifty toss-up race. At least that's what we thought.

The plan was for McCain to give a talk at my campaign rally and then do some media interviews. Among those joining McCain and me on the rally stage were Lindsey Graham, Governor Jeb Bush, and Rep. Tom Davis, the chairman of the NRCC.

The first part of our plan went smoothly. McCain sang my praises to the crowd, urged them to vote for me, and then patiently signed autographs. So far, so good.

The second part was not so smooth. I joined McCain inside the Straight Talk Express bus, which had been plastered with Keller campaign signs inside and out, for a round of media interviews. Right off the bat, a newspaper reporter asked McCain a loaded question: "Ric Keller opposes your campaign finance legislation. What do you think of that?" (Although I liked some parts of the bill, I felt other parts were unconstitutional because they restricted free speech in violation of the First Amendment.) McCain didn't buy my arguments. He replied, "Ric is a great guy. But he is full of sh*t. The arguments against my bill are total bullsh*t."

I secretly thought, *Holy crap! McCain is saying I'm "full of sh*t" the day before my election?! When the race is tied?! Are you kidding me?!* Rather than hit the panic button, I simply laughed off his comments and joked, "Oh well, this is the Straight Talk Express, after all!" I didn't sleep well that night. I imagined the worst. I could wake up on the morning of Election Day with the newspaper headline that read:

"MCCAIN SAYS KELLER FULL OF SH*T"

Luckily, the paper didn't run the headline, and there was no mention at all of any "colorful" language. Just the opposite. There was just a nice photo of McCain and me at the rally.

As to the aftermath, I won the next day, 51–49 percent, and the US Supreme Court agreed with me and declared those parts of the McCain-Feingold finance bill to be unconstitutional. McCain was a bona fide war hero—but he was not a lawyer.

There were no hard feelings. Just the opposite, even though it caused me a little temporary stress and sleep loss, I had total respect for how McCain always had the courage to speak his truth—even when it wasn't convenient. Eight years later, I was proud to be one of the first Florida congressmen to endorse John McCain in the crowded Florida Republican primary for president versus Rudy Giuliani, Mitt Romney, and three others. McCain won the Florida primary and the Republican nomination in 2008—but ultimately lost the general election to Barack Obama.

With straight-talking Senator John McCain after a campaign rally.

Wall Street Bailout

"Wall Street got drunk, and we got the hangover," said President George W. Bush in summarizing the 2008 Financial Crisis. Wall Street firms made billions of dollars off mortgage-backed securities until the house of cards came crashing down. In September 2008, they asked Congress to bail them out.

The origin of the problem is well-known. Lenders gave adjustable-rate mortgages to almost anybody, including the so-called subprime borrowers whose low credit scores made them a higher risk. A perfect storm happened when home prices dropped, adjustable-rate mortgages went up, and subprime borrowers could no longer afford their mortgages. Unable to refinance or sell, they defaulted in huge numbers.

This created a huge problem for Wall Street investment banks, like Lehman Brothers and Goldman Sachs, that had purchased large numbers of mortgages from lenders, repackaged them, and converted them into complex mortgage-backed security assets that they aggressively sold and from which they made billions.

"Rainy Days and Mondays"

"Rainy days and Mondays always get me down," sang the Carpenters. When it comes to the Wall Street bailout, three Mondays in September 2008 got me down. The first Monday was September 15, 2008, when Lehman Brothers, one of the country's largest investment banks, filed for bankruptcy. It was the biggest bankruptcy in US history and was triggered by the unprecedented losses it took from the subprime mortgage crisis. It was the big first domino to fall.

The second Monday was on September 22, 2008, when I walked into my DC office and saw a three-page Wall Street bailout bill on my desk. It proposed that Congress give a jaw-dropping $700 billion "blank check" to the secretary of the treasury to deal with the sub-prime mortgage crisis.

The bailout bill, officially called the Economic Stabilization Act of 2008, created a program called the Troubled Asset Relief Program, or TARP, that would supposedly use $700 billion to purchase the toxic assets. However, the bare-bones bill gave complete discretion to the treasury secretary as to how to spend the money and said his decisions would be "non-reviewable" by any court or administrative agency.

The third Monday was September 29, 2008, the day we voted on the Wall Street bailout.

Paulson: A Lot of Explaining to Do

I had met with Treasury Secretary Hank Paulson a few months earlier in the Oval Office with President Bush. It was a happier occasion. We were there for the signing ceremony on one of my higher education bills. I respected him (and still do). He was bright, earnest, and well-qualified. He held an MBA from Harvard and had been CEO of Goldman Sachs.

But still, asking members of Congress to sign off on giving $700 billion in taxpayer money to the Wall Street firms that created the crisis seemed like one hell of a stretch to me. Paulson had a lot of explaining to do in order to get the House Republicans on board for the big vote.

A Tough Meeting

On the morning of Wednesday, September 24, 2008 (five days before the vote), Secretary Paulson and Ben Bernanke, the chairman of the Federal Reserve, met with the GOP House members behind closed doors inside the Cannon Caucus Room.

Paulson painted an incredibly bleak picture. He told us that he needed $700 billion, that he needed it now, and that the money would be used to buy toxic mortgages. If we didn't give him the money, "Two weeks from now, you won't be able to get a car loan or boat loan," he said.

There were microphones on both sides of the ornate room. I was the first one to ask Secretary Paulson a question that morning.

Me: "Mr. Secretary, you said people won't be able to get a car loan or boat loan two weeks from now. What is the percentage chance of that actually happening?"

Paulson: "We don't know."

Me: "Well, is it a five percent chance? Sixty percent chance?"

Paulson: "Wish I could tell you. We don't know."

Me: "If Congress gave you the $700 billion, would we avoid the recession?"

Paulson: "We don't know."

There were many other tough questions.

How do we tell regular, hardworking people back home that their tax dollars should go to the Wall Street firms that made billions and caused the problem?

Are we rewarding the misconduct from Wall Street? Wouldn't they be more likely to engage in future risky behavior if they know the government is going to bail them out?

How do we know the money will be spent to buy "toxic assets"? What if the corporations who accept federal bailout dollars pay out fat bonuses or give golden parachutes?

Paulson had a tough assignment. There's a reason "Don't kill the messenger" is a common phrase. From being inside the room, I got the sense that two-thirds or more of the House GOP members, including me, would vote no on the Wall Street bailout.

House Minority Leader John Boehner could sense it, too. He would vote for it but called the bill a "sh*t sandwich." Secretary Paulson also knew the meeting was a fiasco. He later wrote about it in his memoir, *On the Brink*:

> "I was not looking forward to meeting with the entire House Republican Conference. Knowing how difficult this meeting would be, I asked Ben Bernanke to accompany me. We would have to make them see the real danger for the average American. . . . They lined up ten-deep on both sides of the room, waiting for a microphone, and blasted us. They could not be persuaded to support TARP. It was an untenable situation."

Later that night, President Bush gave a nationally televised address. Although it was a good speech, it did not persuade me or many other skeptical House Republican colleagues to vote yes. Paulson knew it, too. He said: "Before I went to bed that night, I watched President Bush address the nation. . . . It was his most substantive address yet on the financial crisis, and it was well-delivered, but the last thought I had before I fell asleep was that even a speech by the president wouldn't be able to sway the House Republicans."[93]

"The Stock Market Is Going to Crash"

Prior to the September 29, 2008, vote, the major Republican leaders (President Bush, John Boehner, Mitch McConnell), the GOP nominee for president (John McCain), the Democratic leaders (Nancy Pelosi, Harry Reid), and the Democratic nominee for president (Barack Obama) ALL publicly endorsed the bill.

The media, Wall Street insiders, and most of the public thought passage of the Wall Street bailout bill was a done deal. Essentially, with all the big guns on board, they assumed the House Republicans would follow their leaders like sheep.

However, they weren't inside that closed-door meeting with me, Paulson, and the House Republicans a few days earlier. Trouble was brewing.

On the morning of the big vote, Monday, September 29, 2008, I had breakfast with a Democrat congressman from Pennsylvania in the Capitol:

"So you guys are voting for this thing today, huh?" he asked.

"Nope," I said. His jaw hit the floor.

"Aren't Boehner and Bush supporting it?"

"Yes, but I'm guessing at least two-thirds of us will vote no."

"How many Dems will vote for it?" I asked.

"A slight majority."

I quickly crunched the numbers. And then it hit me. "Oh my God, this bill is going down. Wall Street has no idea. The stock market is going to crash."

Sure enough, that afternoon, at 2:07 PM, the final vote was cast. It failed by a margin of 228 to 205. Two-thirds of the House Republicans had voted against it, and 60 percent of the Democrats had voted in favor of it. The stock market went into free fall. The Dow dropped 770 points. Up to that point, it was the largest single-day point loss in history.[94]

The Second Vote

The White House knew the Senate was not the problem; it was the House. Two days later, on Wednesday, October 1, 2008, the Senate passed the bill 74 to 25.

The administration had to try again in the House. The House leadership scheduled a second vote for Friday, October 3. The arm-twisting that went on between the first and second vote was a sight to see. For example, if you were on an "A" committee or were from a "safe" district, there was no question that the leadership expected you to vote for this bill. Dozens of members switched their votes, and it passed overwhelmingly 263 to 171 on October 3, 2008. The president signed it into law that same day.

I held firm and voted no both times. I didn't relish the idea of ticking off so many of my big donors, all my party leaders, and the president (who all insisted I vote for it), but if I didn't have the courage to do what I felt was right, then why be there in the first place?

At the same time, I really admire the courage of Secretary Paulson for coming into the lion's den that day and having to take tough questions from me and many others. While I may not have agreed with him, I have total respect for people who say their truth and stick with it.

The meltdown of the economy one month before the election contributed to the political wave that completely transferred control of the House, Senate, and White House to the other party. Those of us in swing seats were all tossed out.

I didn't like the idea of losing my job. But I still liked myself for trying to do the right thing. Maybe I was right. The country still went into a deep recession, and millions lost their jobs. Maybe I was wrong. The companies that got the money ultimately paid it all back, and perhaps the recession could have been even worse.

I honestly don't know. What I do know is that all of us should have the courage to do what we believe is right. And let the chips fall where they fall.

Be Bold: Lead Your Team, Fire Toxic People

Nobody is purely "self-made." You will need an organized team working in harmony toward a common goal. The head of a company needs operations, finance, marketing, sales, technical experts, and other functions. A politician needs a campaign manager, press secretary, grassroots director, pollster, TV ad person, and social media expert. When these minds are coordinated in a spirit of harmony and working toward a common goal, the collective energy force is very powerful—far more than merely an aggregate of individuals. Napoleon Hill referred to this as a "Mastermind" in his classic book, *Think and Grow Rich*.

It's your job to see to it that your inner circle works together in a spirit of harmony toward a common goal. It only takes one a**hole to ruin the group dynamic. For example, I once had a guy working for me who was excellent at the technical part of his job. He was always nice enough to me. But five of my employees came to see me as a group one day and told me they were all considering quitting because he was frequently a jerk to them when I wasn't around. They gave me some disturbing examples. This was a toxic situation. He was never that way with me, and he did the technical part of his job well, but I let him go. The team ran smoothly after that.

How one treats other people is their most valuable currency. Everyone is nice to their boss. Everyone is nice to someone they need something from. But how does a person treat people with less power when they think nobody is watching? You can quickly tell a lot about a person's character by how they treat people with less power. For example, if a person is rude to the waiter, they are probably a jerk. Surround yourself with good people.

I've seen the opposite too many times: companies, organizations, and teams tolerating bad behavior because of the person's ability to generate revenue, other business skills, longevity with the organization, or even simply the leader's unwillingness to create conflict.

While jerks in the workplace (or your personal life) can theoretically change their ways, my observation is that it is temporary, and many go back to their old ways without a sincere willingness to change and without serious coaching and other interventions. It requires energy for toxic people to fake being nice. Letting people go is unpleasant (for you and them), and it's easy to put it off. But it's weak to allow your Mastermind and other team members' happiness and productivity to be negatively impacted because you want to avoid confrontation.

The moral of the story is do not allow any toxic or negative people inside your inner circle, and if they slip in somehow, your job is to have the boldness to take action—and let them go.

TAKEAWAY

The secret to connecting with people is having the courage to be authentic, truthful, and vulnerable. It is your job as a leader to make sure your inner circle works together in a spirit of harmony toward a common goal.

CHAPTER 13
Civility in Relationships

"The challenge of leadership is to be strong, but not rude;
be kind, but not weak; be bold, but not bully; be thoughtful,
but not lazy; be humble, but not timid; be proud, but
not arrogant; have humor, but without folly."

—Jim Rohn

While great leaders must be honest, direct, and bold as described in the prior chapter, they also understand the importance of civility and courtesy. Tom Osborne, the legendary former coach of the Nebraska Cornhuskers football team, leads by example on this issue better than anyone I've ever met.

Osborne and I were elected to Congress in 2000 and sat next to each other on the House Education Committee for six years. I would describe him as a truly unique leader for at least three reasons. First, not too many football coaches have a PhD in educational psychology.

Second, he's not a rah-rah kind of guy. I would describe Coach as quiet, soft-spoken, calm, humble, and a good listener. He didn't talk much during our committee hearings, but when he did, you could hear a pin drop. Everybody stopped what they were doing and listened.

Third, he truly is one of the greatest college football coaches of all time, right up there with Bear Bryant and Bobby Bowden. The Nebraska Cornhuskers were national champions three times in his final four seasons. His teams during his final five years had a combined record of 60–3. And in more than twenty-five years at Nebraska, he had a career record of 255–49–3 (.836). It's no surprise that the College Football Hall of Fame waived its three-year waiting period and inducted him right away.

We shared a passion for mentoring. We worked together on legislation called the Mentoring for Success Act, which was signed into law by President George W. Bush as part of his education reform legislation, and we served on the Mentoring Caucus.

I'm a huge college football fan, and Coach Osborne was kind enough to give me his take on many of my college football questions, including the topics of recruiting, pre-game locker room speeches, and his friendship with Bobby Bowden of Florida State University.

Bobby Bowden was the second-winningest football coach in major college history and had two national championships. Bowden was such an admirer of Osborne that he wrote the foreword for the biography of Tom Osborne, called *Heart of a Husker*, by Mike Babcock.[95]

In the foreword, Bowden said the first time he personally met Tom Osborne was when Florida State played Nebraska in Lincoln in

1980. Bowden heard a knock on his dressing room door before the game. He opened it up, and there was Osborne himself, decked out in red. Osborne asked, "Did y'all get in okay? Is everything okay? Is there anything I can do for you?"

Bowden was impressed. Although Nebraska was favored to win that game, the Seminoles snuck out with a victory. After the game, as Bowden and the FSU team walked off the field, the Nebraska fans stood up and clapped for them. Bowden said the courtesy was a reflection of Tom. Bowden was so impressed he wrote an open letter complimenting Nebraska and its fans, and the letter was published in the Nebraska newspapers.[96]

FSU played Nebraska for the national championship in the Orange Bowl in 1993. At the time, neither Osborne nor Bowden had won a national championship. FSU won. A few months later, Osborne came to Tallahassee, Florida, for a few days to learn what types of things FSU was doing. They had suppers together, and Bowden even let Osborne sit in on staff meetings.[97]

After that, Nebraska won three national championships in the next four years. I once asked Coach about the rumor that Nebraska recruited faster players based on advice he got from Bobby Bowden on that trip. He had a humorous reply. "Ric, I'm no rocket scientist, but I'm pretty sure I already knew you've got to be fast to play football."

In his excellent book, *Tom Osborne on Leadership*, Pat Williams interviewed dozens of former players to learn about Osborne's leadership style. The interviews revealed at least four things that made the players respect the coach so much. First, Osborne treated the freshmen walk-ons with the same respect as the All-Americans. He knew their names and took an interest in them. Second, the coach would say, "Now, fellas, after you knock your man down, make sure you pick him up." Third, "Coach never yelled at us or embarrassed us in front of our teammates. If he needed to address an issue, he'd do it behind closed doors." Fourth, "He spread the credit for our successes and took the blame for our failures."[98]

If you want to be a leader in politics, sports, or business, I can't think of a better person to emulate than Coach Osborne.

A Harvard Lesson in Civility

On November 30, 2020, I wrote an article for the *Harvard Crimson* that strongly encouraged newly elected members of Congress to attend the bipartisan orientation program sponsored by the Harvard Kennedy School's Institute of Politics (formally titled the Bipartisan Program for Newly Elected Members of Congress) because of the positive role it plays in fostering bipartisan civility, which matters now more than ever.[99]

It was the twentieth anniversary of my attendance at the Harvard Kennedy School's freshman orientation program, as I journeyed to Cambridge in December 2000 as a newly elected member of the House of Representatives from Florida.

Regrettably, there has been some controversy about the Harvard Kennedy School's freshman orientation program over the years. For example, in 1994, all Republicans boycotted the event, claiming that Harvard was too left-leaning. In 2018, some Democrats attending the orientation complained there were CEO speakers but not enough labor union speakers.

These complaints all missed the mark. They underestimated the value of a representative keeping an open mind to all sides. After all, would it kill a Republican to hear what a left-leaning Harvard professor has to say about improving access to higher education for poorer students? Would it be so bad for a Democrat to listen to what a right-leaning CEO has to say about how to create more jobs in the private sector?

The program I attended in 2000 attracted a broad bipartisan group of new members from Florida to California, many of whom have since become well-known. The attendees included the then-youngest member of Congress, Adam H. Putnam (R-FL), future Trump Impeachment Manager Adam B. Schiff (D-CA), future Majority Leader Eric I. Cantor (R-VA), and future Senators Jeffry L. Flake (R-AZ), and Mark S. Kirk (R-IL). I made productive use of my time at Harvard in the midst of such good company.

For example, I drafted my first piece of bipartisan legislation at the Kennedy School's orientation. I used spare minutes between panels to write up a bill to expand Pell Grants, which I filed on my first day in Congress. President George W. Bush later gave me the pen he used to sign my Pell Grant legislation into law, and I was promoted to chairman of the House Higher Education Subcommittee.

Over four days, we received policy briefings from prominent experts, including Cabinet secretaries, senior White House aides, business leaders, and Harvard faculty on a wide variety of topics—including the federal budget, foreign policy, and education reform—to help us hit the ground running when we arrived in Washington.

One of the more interesting moments for me was asking former Treasury Secretary Robert Rubin questions about interest rates. Rubin was very bright and well-qualified. He had degrees from Harvard, Yale, and the London School of Economics and had been chairman of Goldman Sachs before becoming secretary of the treasury.

At one of our briefings, I asked Rubin:

Me: "What, if anything, can Congress do to help keep long-term interest rates low?"

Rubin: "Reduce budget deficits."

Me: "Lower deficits foster lower interest rates?"

Rubin: "Yes."

Me: "Remember when Jimmy Carter was president and we had 22 percent interest rates?"

Rubin: "Yes."

Me: "And then during the Reagan years, we had a military buildup that doubled the budget deficit—and yet the interest rates were cut in half, correct?"

Rubin: "Correct."

Me: "Okay, how do you explain that?"

Rubin: "It's very complicated."

Me: "Thank you. I'm still confused—but on a much higher plane."

At Harvard, panel discussion topics included relations between Congress and the White House, and speakers like David R. Gergen (a White House adviser for Presidents Bill Clinton, Ronald Reagan, Gerald Ford, and Richard Nixon), Kenneth M. Duberstein (Ronald Reagan's chief of staff), and Anne L. Wexler (an assistant to Jimmy Carter).

Wexler gave particularly sage advice. "Always remember that in Washington, there are no permanent friends and no permanent enemies," she said. "Civility is the watchword." As someone who served eight years in Congress, I can tell you that she was correct.

The 1994 GOP members who boycotted might have learned a thing or two from Harvard professors. Who knows? I sure did. In the future, I hope that the newly elected members of Congress will give civility a chance.

Bushes and Kennedys

In May 2008, I was invited by President George W. Bush to come to the Oval Office to attend a signing ceremony for a higher education bill I had co-sponsored. I arrived a little early. Senator Ted Kennedy, the bill's Senate sponsor, also got there a bit early. President Bush invited Senator Kennedy and me to join him in the Oval Office as we waited for some others to arrive.

After we walked in, the president walked us over to his desk and said, "Ric, this is the same desk that Ted's brother used when he was president." (The desk used by President John F. Kennedy—called the "Resolute" desk—had been a gift from the queen of England.)

Attending the Oval Office signing ceremony for the higher education bill I co-sponsored.

Then, pointing under the desk, Bush continued: "And this is the same spot where that iconic photograph of little John Jr. (nearly three years old) was taken as he crawled under the desk." Bush then delivered the punch line. "We are now going to reenact that famous scene by having Ted crawl under the desk." Senator Kennedy, who was a well-nourished man (about six foot two and about 275 pounds), laughed heartily. I did, too.

I tell this story because it illustrates that behind closed doors, even the leaders of the two biggest political dynasties, despite being on the opposite ends of the political spectrum, are civil. In fact, in November 2001, it was President George W. Bush who entered an Executive Order that named the Justice Department headquarters after Robert F. Kennedy. At the ceremony, many members of the Kennedy family listened as President Bush spoke glowingly about Robert Kennedy, and RFK's son, former Congressman Joseph P. Kennedy II, hailed President Bush a profile in leadership.[100]

Why is that a good thing? Why would people with opposite views still treat each other with respect and courtesy? Aside from being the right thing to do, President Bush and Senator Kennedy were practical politicians who found common ground on issues where they needed each other, such as education reform and immigration. A person may be your opponent, but that doesn't make them your enemy.

A Classy Electoral College Certification

As someone who was born and educated in Tennessee, I followed Al Gore's successful career from the beginning. Like me, Gore and his mom attended Vanderbilt Law School. (His mom graduated, but Gore left early to run for Congress.)

I first "bumped into" Gore—literally—at Vanderbilt when I was a law student, and he was a senator. After class one day, I pushed open a wooden door to exit the lecture hall, and the other side of the door gently bumped into Gore's back as he was giving an interview to a TV station. "I'm so sorry, Senator. I didn't see you," I said. He was cool about it. "It's quite all right," he said, smiling.

Ten years later, I was standing near Gore once again—this time inside the Chamber of the House of Representatives. I was a newly elected member of Congress, and he was the vice president presiding over the Joint Session of Congress to certify the electoral college votes.

Since the vice president also serves as the president of the Senate, Gore was placed in the highly unusual position of certifying his own defeat.

Normally, congressional certification of the electoral college is quick and routine. But several Democratic House members had told the media in advance that they were going to try to use procedural maneuvers to block the counting of Florida's twenty-five electoral votes. That meant that even though the House members were trying to help him, Gore would have to rule them "out of order" and bring the gavel down to silence them.

Gore handled it with grace and humor. For example, when California's fifty-four electoral votes were awarded to him, Gore playfully pumped his fist in the air. Later, when Rep. Jesse Jackson, Jr., (D-IL) objected to counting Florida's twenty-five electoral votes, Gore said: "The chair thanks the gentleman from Illinois, but, hey." We all erupted in laughter. Rep. Alcee Hastings (D-FL) called out to Gore, "We did all we could." Gore smiled and replied, "The chair thanks the gentleman from Florida."

After the votes were received, Gore read out the numbers that showed his 271 to 266 electoral college defeat. To win, a presidential candidate needs 270 electoral votes. "May God bless our new president and new vice president, and may God bless the United States of America," Gore said. We gave him a standing ovation.

Gore then gaveled the joint session to a close, shook hands with us, and signed a few autographs.

Of course, Mike Pence would be placed in the same role twenty years later, on January 6, 2021, and we saw what a lack of civility looked like during the insurrection. Our country is better than that. The sooner we can get back to treating each other with civility and respect, the better.

TAKEAWAY

Civility, courtesy, and respect are the watchwords of leadership at the highest levels. Speak your truth but do so in a way that does not hurt the other person's self-esteem. Your opponent today may be your ally tomorrow.

CHAPTER 14
Humor and Humility

"There is nothing in the world so irresistibly contagious
as laughter and good humor."
—Charles Dickens

You can do everything you think you are supposed to do, but things will not always go right. You'll make mistakes, you'll be criticized, you'll be embarrassed, you'll fail, and situations won't always turn out the way you expected. Having a sense of humor and humility—being able to laugh at yourself and at life, find humor in little moments, and not take yourself too seriously—help put life in perspective. I've had to constantly rely on this; it helps you survive and makes life more fun too.

Once I got to Washington, I quickly saw firsthand how political leaders could disarm and charm others simply by being able to laugh at themselves and at life. In this chapter, I share some of these funny DC stories that I only tell my friends.

Sonny and Monica

For example, on my first day in Congress, I had a memorable conversation with an elderly congressman from Alabama during an underground train ride between the Capitol and Rayburn House Office Building. With a thick Southern accent, he introduced himself. "I'm Sonny Callahan from Alabama."

I said, "Sonny Callahan? I read the *Starr Report*, and it said that when Bill Clinton was having his intimate encounter with Monica Lewinsky, he was on the telephone talking to a congressman from Alabama named Sonny Callahan. Is that you?"[101]

He replied, "Yeah, it always makes me so mad, too. Nobody ever asks me what I was doing when I was talking to him!"

Mike and Money Shots

Also, during my first week, I was assigned to the Judiciary Committee and seated next to a fellow freshman named Mike Pence. We became friends, and for eight years, we would swap jokes. My jokes were usually R-rated; Mike's were G-rated.

On one occasion, while telling Mike the punchline of a joke, I said, "Mike, here is the money shot." Mike did not fully understand the origin of the term *money shot*. He went back to Indiana and proceeded to use the term "money shot" in several of his speeches . . . town halls, Rotary clubs, chambers of commerce-type meetings, and so on . . . money shot, money shot, money shot.

After one of these speeches, a guy asked Pence if he knew what that meant. Mike said, "It's when Michael Jordan hits the game-winning shot, and that's why they pay him the big money."

The guy said, "No, it isn't. Who told you that term?"

Pence said, "Ric Keller."

The guy said, "Ask Ric Keller what it means."

A few days later, on the floor of the House of Representatives, Mike walked over to me and asked, "What is a money shot?" I had to tell him the truth.

"Well, Mike, the term 'money shot' comes from the world of adult films . . . it's typically the final scene."

He put his face in his hands and said, "Oh no . . ." The key thing is what happened next. Did he crawl up into a fetal position, hide in the closet, and never show his face again? No, he laughed . . . laughed hard . . . biggest laugh I've ever seen from him. It was 100 percent my fault, not his. He did not know what it meant, yet he was sturdy enough to laugh at himself and the situation.

Mike Pence and I became friends after serving in the same freshman class in Congress.

Sleepless in DC

Members of Congress do not get any stipends or living expenses in connection with their time in Washington, DC. Consequently, about seventy members live in their offices and take their showers in the House gymnasium to save money, which I did in my last two terms.

I slept on a rollaway cot I kept in my office closet. My first night on the office cot was memorable. I was awakened at 3 AM by loud rap music ("Baby got back!") blasted from a janitor's boom box as he mopped the fourth floor of the Cannon House Office. I had to get earplugs to block the music at night, which also blocked me from hearing the damn alarm clock go off in the morning. So much for the "glamorous" life.

"Do I Know You?"

As a member of Congress, my face is vaguely recognizable to people in my hometown, but often they don't know *how* they know me. Here's an actual conversation I had:

"How do I know you?" asked the constituent.

I jokingly replied, "I've been on *America's Most Wanted* a few times."

"Seriously, did we go to Colonial High School together?"

"No, I went to Boone."

"Were you a bartender at Big Daddy's?"

"Nope."

"So how do I know you?"

"I'm not sure. Perhaps, maybe because I'm your congressman?"

"Yes. That's it. You look fatter on TV."

"Thank you . . . I think."

Kids and Seniors

Kids and seniors say the darndest things. I attended dozens of town hall meetings at senior centers and made over fifty visits to schools. There were some funny moments.

My favorite incident at a senior center was when an elderly man blamed me for putting Martha Stewart in prison.

By way of background, in 2004, Martha Stewart, the well-known

TV personality and author, had a highly publicized trial and was found guilty of a felony regarding statements she allegedly made about a stock trading deal.[102]

She served five months in a federal prison in West Virginia. Her nickname in prison was M. Diddy. Shortly after M. Diddy began her sentence, I held a senior citizen town hall meeting in Lake County, Florida (just outside of Orlando). At the meeting, an elderly gentleman, who appeared to be about ninety years old, slowly walked up to the microphone.

Senior: "Congressman, I'm so mad at you! I can hardly see straight!"

Me: "Oh man, what did I do?" (I had to smile.)

Senior: "The way you put Martha Stewart in jail!"

Me: "Wait. What? Me?" (I had never even met Martha Stewart.)

Senior: "All these violent criminals are on the loose. And you guys are going after this poor lady? You should be ashamed of yourselves!"

Me: "Anything else?" (I let elderly people talk as long as they want.)

Senior: "I'm just getting started."

Me: "Okay. Go ahead."

Senior: "Just leave her alone. It's a waste of taxpayer money. Now I'm done."

Me: "Thank you, sir. There are three branches of government. I'm in the legislative branch. I didn't have anything to do with Martha Stewart's criminal prosecution. It's the other branches of government that handle this."

Senior: "Oh, you're all in it together. One big government. You know it, and I know it!" (Clearly, it was time for me to throw in the towel.)

Me: "Sir, it won't happen again."

Senior: "Now that's what I'm talking about! Thank you!"

Me: "You're welcome."

I kept my "promise." Martha Stewart never went back to prison.

Kids ask the funniest questions, especially children in kindergarten through third grade.

Typically, the teacher says something like, "We have been studying about the government. Today, our special guest is Congressman Ric Keller. He can answer any of your questions about the government. Please raise your hand if you have any questions."

Some of the questions they asked are:

"Did you see the movie *Jaws*?"

"Wouldn't you be scared to get bit by a shark?"

"You said you played football. Were you the shortest kid on the team?"

"Do you make as much money as an Orlando Magic player?"

"Do you have a limo?"

"Are you famous?"

"Do you live in a mansion?"

"Did you hate homework, too?"

"Do you like kickball?"

"Did you ever play dodgeball—and did you get hit?"

"Still the One"

Of all the DC stories, this is still the one I love the most. In October 2007, I traveled to Iraq on a fact-finding trip as part of a small congressional delegation that included Rep. John Hall (D-NY). Before pursuing a political career, John Hall had been a member of the rock band Orleans and was co-writer of the band's smash hit "Still the One."

In Baghdad, I slept at Saddam Hussein's palace. They warned us not to drink the contaminated water, but I forgot. Not too long after, I found myself in a foreign hospital, surrounded by doctors and diagnosed with *E. coli* poisoning. While I was in the hospital, Hall performed for the troops, and I missed it.

Eventually, our small delegation flew back to America in a large Air Force jet. As we made our way over the Atlantic Ocean, John Hall walked up to the front of the jet where I was sitting and asked if I was feeling okay. I said, "Yeah, but I'm bummed I missed hearing your songs." He replied, "I've got my guitar with me. Why don't you grab a couple crew members and meet me in the middle of the plane, and I'll play them for you."

It was a magical moment. I was in a jet flying over the Atlantic Ocean, and a famous musician was performing a private concert for me. He played all the hits, including "Still the One."

After he was done playing, I asked him to tell me the story behind the song. He told me that he wrote the song with his wife, Johanna, after a couple they were friends with made the surprise announcement they were going to divorce. I asked him about that.

Me: "Did you play it for those friends?"

Hall: "Yeah."

Me: "Did they like it?"

Hall: "Yeah, they loved it."

Me: "Did they stay together?"

Hall: "No, they got a divorce anyway."

Me: "How's your co-writer wife doing these days?"

Hall: "Oh, we got a divorce, too."

I had to laugh.

M&M's Jail

President George W. Bush graciously invited me to ride with him on Air Force One four times. On my first trip as a freshman, I took a seat onboard and quickly noticed a box of M&M's that had a gold presidential seal on them laying on the table in front of me. There were also some trinkets with the Air Force One logo. I faced a difficult moral decision: *Should I steal these M&M's?*

It almost felt like the devil was whispering in my ear. "Steal them. You will *never* be on this plane again. You shouldn't even be here now, you Wendy's reject. Eat them. It's not like that *diet* is working out for you anyway, fat boy. Steal them, eat them." I ate them.

I think the flight attendant might have seen me. A few minutes later, he walked over and handed me a gift bag filled with M&M's and Air Force One swag—coffee cups, pens, pencils, napkins, and other trinkets. The look on his face said, "Here you go, Congressman. You don't have to steal them. We'll just give them to you." I was an inch away from going to M&M's jail. Luckily, there was no evidence. M&M's melt in your mouth, not in your hands.

The Queens' Room

President George W. Bush and First Lady Laura Bush invited a small group of House members over to their personal residence in the White House for dinner. Afterward, the First Lady asked if we wanted a tour. Of course, we said yes.

She then gave us a tour of the second-floor family quarters of the White House, which includes two guest rooms. The most famous of these guest rooms is the Lincoln Bedroom. Although not as well-known, the second guest room directly across from the Lincoln

Bedroom, called the Queens' Bedroom, is one of the prettiest rooms in the mansion.

As our guide, the First Lady was quite knowledgeable and told us interesting historical facts about each room on the tour. The president quietly stood back and let her shine.

When we entered the Queens' Bedroom, Laura Bush only got out the first few words of her story—"The Queens' Bedroom gets its name from . . ."—when her cell phone rang.

"I'm so sorry," she said. "It's my daughter. I've got to take this. George, will you take over?"

The president slowly made his way from the back of the group to the center of the Queens' Bedroom. Then, in his Texas twang, he kicked into tour-guide mode. He wasn't as up to speed on the historical details as the First Lady.

"This here's the Queens' Room. Some kind of queen stayed here. I don't know. England. Or Norway. Or something like that. That's, um, the queen's bed. Over there's the queen's window. This is the, uh, queen's luggage." He had a funny little smirk on his face that seemed to say, "Listen, y'all know I don't know sh*t about this room, so cut me a break."

Just then, Laura returned and gracefully took over. "George, did I hear you say Norway? That's good, honey." And then she gave us the real scoop with accurate details. "The Queens' Room gets its name from the many royal visitors who stayed here, including the queens from Spain, the Netherlands, Norway, Greece, and Great Britain. Both Queen Elizabeth (the Queen Mother) and Queen Elizabeth II stayed here. Winston Churchill stayed here as well." And, just like that, we were back on track.

Seeing the president interact with his family members, joke around with us, or commit the occasional gaffe makes you realize something. Presidents are people, too.

Barbara Bush

I initially met Barbara Bush in 2000 when she and her husband, President George H.W. Bush, did a campaign event with me in Orlando days before my first election. About five years later, it was March 18, 2005, and President George W. Bush was flying to Orlando to do a senior citizen town hall meeting. The president invited three congressmen from Florida and me to join him and his mom for the ride on Air Force One.

After we were in the air, President Bush invited us to take a seat on the couch inside his flying "Oval Office" while he and his mom had lunch. Watching the two of them rib each other was hysterical.

Attending a meeting in the flying Oval Office on Air Force One. Seated from left to right: President George W. Bush, First Lady Barbara Bush, Rep. Dave Weldon, Rep, Adam Putnam, me, and Rep. Tom Feeney.

For example, after one of his mom's many good-natured barbs, Bush said to us, "Don't listen to this eighty-year-old woman; she's crazy." After which she turned to us and said (with a smile), "Don't laugh at his jokes; you will only encourage him." Here he was, the president of the United States, and yet his mom still treated him like a mischievous six-year-old boy.

After we arrived at the event, the playful banter between mother and son continued in front of the crowd. Mrs. Bush introduced her son at the event and said, "When my world was nothing but peanut butter and jelly sandwiches, Little League games, and brownies, I just, frankly, hoped he'd grow up. . . . Tenaciousness is what you want in a president. It's not what you want in a six-year-old."

The forty-third president relayed a funny story about their final in-person meeting in the hospital before she passed away in 2018. Barbara Bush said, "Doctor, do you want to know why George W is the way he is? It's because I drank and smoked when I was pregnant with him."[103] It's easy to see why the American people loved the former First Lady. We all did. RIP, Barbara Bush.

"Because We Said So!"

Justice Antonin Scalia was quick-witted. I got a glimpse of Scalia's wit one morning over coffee when he was a guest at our weekly "Theme Team" meeting. (The Theme Team was an informal group of GOP members who convened every Thursday morning with newsmakers and well-known individuals for coffee and interesting conversation.) One of my colleagues, Rep. Jean Schmidt (R-OH), requested an explanation regarding two conflicting Supreme Court rulings about whether it was okay to display the Ten Commandments on government property.

Schmidt: "Explain to me why the Supreme Court said it was okay to display the Commandments in Texas but not in Kentucky."

Scalia: "Why?"

Schmidt: "Yes, why?"

Scalia (smiling): "Because we said so, that's why."

The room erupted in laughter. Scalia was just kidding. On the same day, the Court had handed down two conflicting 5–4 opinions. Scalia voted consistently to allow the display of the Commandments in both Texas and Kentucky—and had even personally written the dissenting opinion in the Kentucky case. Still, his lighthearted approach won over the audience much better than any complicated legal lecture.

The Blue Patch

The other thing I loved to do at elementary schools was pass out the Presidential Physical Fitness Awards. The award consisted of a round blue patch and a certificate "signed" by the president of the United States. To win the prize, a student must score in the eighty-fifth percentile or above in various skill tests, including the fifty-yard dash, pull ups, shuttle run, six-hundred-yard run, and broad jump.

I visited Hillcrest Elementary School in Orlando, Florida, and brought Dot Richardson with me. She was the perfect choice. Dot had won two Olympic gold medals and was the vice chairman of the President's Council on Physical Fitness.

The event went smoothly . . . at first. Dot and I passed out the blue patches to the winners. Even better, I listened as Dot gave an inspirational talk to the kids. *Wow, this went great,* I thought. We began to say our goodbyes. And then the school's PE teacher made a surprise announcement to the hundreds of students and parents gathered in attendance for the school's field day activities and awards program.

She had selected the fastest girl and boy in fifth grade to challenge Dot and me to a foot race.

I didn't see this coming. But to be good sports, we accepted the challenge. I remembered the TV game show, *Are You Smarter than a 5th Grader?* This contest would be: "Are You Faster than a 5th Grader?" I didn't know the answers to either question. At the time, I was forty-three, and Dot was forty-six. I was pretty sure that I was faster than a first-grader and slower than a twelfth-grader. But a fifth-grader? That's a gray area.

The PE teacher selected a speed contest called the shuttle run. She placed two wooden blocks about thirty feet apart. The contestants had to run down, pick up the first block, run back, and do it a second time. What should we do? Do we let the kids win or try to outrace them?

With our feet on the starting line, I leaned over and whispered to Dot: "Do we let them win?" Dot, a fierce competitor, said, "No way! I'm going all out." I decided to do the same. (I should mention that this was my strongest event when I was in elementary school.)

The race was over in about ten seconds. Dot and I easily won our respective races. But as soon as we crossed the finish line, many of the parents began booing at us. They apparently thought we were bad sports for not letting the kids win. We went from "hero to zero" in ten seconds.

I won the race but lost the votes. But at least I got the answers to my questions: I was faster than a fifth-grade runner but *dumber* than a fifth-grade politician.

Olympic gold medalist Dot Richardson and I learned a lesson from elementary school students in Orlando.

I've been on top of the world and hit bottom, with lots of ups and downs in between. There was one thing in my life that stayed the same. One source of stability. One life raft that kept me alive. And that was the ability to laugh at myself and put life in perspective.

I mention that because you, too, will have a few ups and downs. Perhaps even now, you're going through something. You may have a job you hate, your boss is a jerk, you're in a toxic personal relationship, you're struggling with your weight, you can't pay your bills, the medical report isn't good, someone you thought was a friend betrayed your trust, you lost a dream job that was central to your identity, you're going through a divorce, or you have to move to a new area where you have no friends or relatives. You wonder if there's any reason for hope.

I get it. I've been there—for all of them. You're going to be okay. God has pulled you through every other adversity, and you will get through this one. The proof is you're still alive. My hope for you is that when you hit the low point, I hope you know it's temporary. I hope you know you're going to be okay. Ten years from now, most of those things will be funny stories at cocktail parties. If you can laugh at yourself and at life, you will be unstoppable.

TAKEAWAY

Don't take yourself too seriously. Your sense of humor and humility will help keep life in perspective, especially when the road gets bumpy.

EPILOGUE:
Bad Advice
on Bear Safety

"Bear eyes can see deeper into your soul
than Deepak Chopra."
—Ethan Nicolle

When I wrote this book's Introduction, my wife was concerned that some people might mistake the "chase the bears" metaphor as bad advice on bear safety and possibly get hurt. As a condition of my marriage, Lori required me to make it clear in this Epilogue that I am not advocating that you chase bears in the forest during your next camping trip.

What should you do if you encounter a bear? The experts say you should use your "bear spray." Pull out your gun. Call for the nearby ranger. Thanks experts, but 99 percent of the time, those options aren't available.

My daughter and I heeding the warning signs about bear activity.

Well, just make yourself look bigger, they say, by waving your arms, pulling your shoulders back, and standing on your tippy-toes. I told my eight-year-old daughter that same advice when she got measured at the carnival ride, and somehow, it didn't work. Besides, you're still *not* bigger than the bear.

I do not hold myself out as an expert. I wanted to learn more about what the "bear safety experts" have to say about bear encounters, so I did some Internet research. Here are five bear safety tips from actual published Internet articles and YouTube videos:

Bear Safety Tips:

Play with her cubs.
Play dead.
Sing a song.
DO feed the bears.
Call the rangers.

Dave Brinnel offered my favorite, albeit unconventional, piece of advice: "An adult black bear can weigh as much as five hundred pounds. But good news. Black bears won't hurt you as long as they believe you are not out to hurt them. So what's the best way to earn their trust? Play with their cubs. Climb on the cubs. Wrestle with them. Make a lot of noise. Slap their furry bottoms. When the mother bear returns, she'll see how much you like her cubs, and she'll become your friend for life."[105]

When he is not giving bear safety tips, Brinnel is a musician, radio host, and ad maker. He played piano at campaign rallies for President Ronald Reagan, gave Rachel Maddow her first job in radio, and made TV commercials for Disney. How can anybody loved by Reagan, Maddow, and Mickey Mouse possibly be wrong? Maybe he's right?

I've encountered black bears in the wild three times. My fight-or-flight instincts kicked in, and I ran like hell. In the heat of the moment, I thought *It's a bear. I'm not a bear. It has the advantage. Bullsh*t, I'm playing dead or singing 'Don't Stop Believin'!' Peace out, bear. I'm running!* (On one of those occasions, the bear was more scared than me and climbed a tree.)

Running is technically the worst thing you can do. You can't outrun a bear. Now, I'm not saying that you *should* run. But what I am saying is that if I were in Las Vegas, I would bet all of my money (and my kids' college fund, too) that you *will* run.

Tom Smith, a bear biologist who spent twenty-one years studying human-bear encounters, says that playing dead is the dumbest thing you could do with black bears: "Black bears only attack to kill, so playing dead with one of those will be facilitated by the fact that you will, in fact, be dead soon enough."[106]

And, finally, there's the "call the rangers" safety tip. Your life turns on what happens in the next thirty seconds. They can't help you in time. "Rangers are just humans with funny hats. There is nothing they can do that you cannot do yourself. The only thing a ranger can do is update the park's 'Days Since a Bear Attack' sign, and that rarely changes from zero," said Ethan Nicolle, author of *Bears Want to Kill You: The Authoritative Guide to Survival in the War Between Man and Bear.*[107]

The bottom line is—whether it is a bear in the woods or a goal on your three-by-five card—you are the one responsible for making things happen. The good news is the world's most powerful goal-setting formula in Chapter 2 gives you the tools you need to get to where you want to be.

I hope you use your gifts, trust your instincts, and don't take yourself too seriously.

The "shadow of the bear" (cover) is a reminder that we are only given a limited amount of time to pursue our dreams. "The bad news is time flies. The good news is you're the pilot," said author Michael Altshuler. Put the destination that YOU want into the autopilot feature (and onto a goal card), and then stay on course, despite any turbulence along the journey.

You will be okay. You will land this plane. Safe travels, my friend.

With a bear hug,

Ric Keller
Winter Park, Florida

Acknowledgments

I am so grateful for the many incredible people who helped bring this book to life. First and foremost, thank you to my wife, Lori. You chased the bears with me, literally and figuratively. I'll always remember sitting with you at our kitchen table for those countless late night coffee-fueled writing sessions. Your inspiration, ideas, wisdom, intuition, candor, editing, humor, and love made the book so much better. This book is as much yours as it is mine.

Thank you to Don Green, the executive director of the Napoleon Hill Foundation, for your years of dedication in helping to bring the timeless wisdom of Napoleon Hill to a new generation, and for kindly introducing me to my literary agent.

Hats off to my literary agent, Dan Strutzel, for taking a chance on a first-time author, for having faith in this book's message from the get-go, and for your relentless effort in making sure *Chase the Bears* found the right publishing home.

A big thank you to Christine Belleris for being the perfect editor for this book. You and the team at HCI books, including Larissa Henoch, Lindsey Mach, Christian Blonshine, and Peter Vegso have my deepest thanks and appreciation.

I want to give shout outs to Jennifer Jas for your excellent proof-reading and copy editing, to Steve Vaughn for your photograph on the book cover, and to Paul Peterzell for letting us publish your touching poem about the Big Tree. And special thanks to the creative website (and musical) genius Ron Passaro, and to Iris Blasi for your guidance with social media and help navigating the book world.

Thank you to everyone I featured in the book. Your incredible stories moved me and will inspire many people for years to come.

I am grateful to my dad, Marv Orenstein, and mom, Lora Keller, along with "Linda Lou," Uncle C.B., Auntie Sue, and my siblings Jack, Caran, Jeff and J.R. for their love and support. Also, a special thank you to my in-laws, Tony and Valerie Spivey, for personally attending my TEDx Talk and for the amazing job you did in raising the love of my life, Lori, to be such a kindhearted soul.

I am so thankful for the incredible children in our blended family. Each of you have your own special and unique gifts that will make the world a better place. Thank you to Nick, Christy, Kaylee, Kate, Allie, Jacob, and Gage, and for their mothers, Cathy, Dee Dee, and Lori.

In many ways, this book took fifty-seven years to write. I want to thank my close friends who provided such wise counsel and support along the journey, including Jason Brodeur, Chris Dorworth, Mike Miller, Stefan Spath, Brian Garrow, Ted Barry, John and Claudia Bachman, Sid and Allie Price, Mary Hayes, William Jeter, Cheryl Mills, Jason Miller, Bryan Malenius, Taylor Ford, and my law partners Chris Hill, Ken Rugh, and Steve Main.

I also want to thank my fellow Angry Unicorns motorcycle "gang" members, especially my co-founders Tom Wert, Gregg Morrell, Carlos Velasco and Joe "The Biker" Darcangelo. Our many memorable rides, from Sturgis, South Dakota, to the Tail of the Dragon in

Tennessee, to Bike Week in Daytona, have given me the headspace to be creative. Also, your good advice, often delivered over a beer at a biker bar, has had such a positive impact on my personal life.

As an old speech communication major, I have an odd hobby of watching and appreciating amazing commencement speeches. Typically, a prominent speaker does it for free and their only goal is to selflessly impart wisdom to a new generation. Once in a while, someone comes along and simply hits it out of the park.

I want the thank and acknowledge the handful of graduation speakers who have inspired me, and millions of others, with their exceptional talks, including: Dolly Parton, Abby Wambach, Oprah Winfrey, J.K. Rowling, Lisa Kudrow, Ellen DeGeneres, Steve Harvey, Steve Jobs, Jim Carrey, Admiral William McRaven, Sanjay Gupta (who kindly let me borrow one of his jokes from his talk at Michigan), James Ryan, George Saunders, Tim Minchin, Larry King, and Steve Carrell. I suspect that some of you may not fully realize the positive impact your words have had on others. Your speeches—along with Brené Brown's TEDx Talk on vulnerability—were all delivered with warmth, humor, and incredible wisdom. Thank you for your willingness to toss down the "rope ladder" of success and try to help others to climb up, too.

Finally, I want to thank you, my reader. I hope this book feels like a huge bear hug. I think there's a reason this book fell into your hands. Your dreams matter! Your gifts matter! You matter! It's not too late. I hope you use your unique gifts, trust your intuition, and chase the bears!

Notes

Introduction

[1] "Shadow of the Bear." www.discoverjacksonnc.com. https://www. discoverjacksonnc.com/attractions/shadow-of-the-bear/

[2] Ibid.

[3] Harvey, S. (2016). Jump. Amistad.

[4] Ibid.

Chapter 1

[5] Dolly Parton commencement address, University of Tennessee, May 9, 2008.

[6] "Dolly Parton reflects on her greatest moments," CMT. com, July 7, 2006. http://www.cmt.com/news/1535871/ dolly-parton-reflects-on-her-greatest-moments/

[7] "Perfect pairing." (2019, Sept. 17). laughlinentertainer.com. http:// laughlinentertainer.com/?p=8217

[8] Dolly Parton commencement address, University of Tennessee, May 9, 2008.

[9] Clouse, A. (2020, July 30). "Dollywood is more popular than Disneyland, according to Tripadvisor." *Knoxville News Sentinel,* https://www.knoxnews.com/story/entertainment/2020/07/30dollywood-ranks-top-10-amusement-parks-us-and-worldwide/5544650002/https://www.celebritynetworth.com/richest-celebrities/singers/dolly-parton-net-worth/. Extracted 2022, February 13. Wendowski, A. (2021, March 14). "Dolly Parton secures 10th Grammy Award with Zach Williams Collaboration." CountryNow. https://countrynow.com/dolly-parton-secures-tenth-grammy-award-with-zach-williams-collaboration/

[10] Jim Carrey commencement address, Maharishi University. March 24, 2014.

[11] Oprah interview of Jim Carrey on October 13, 2011, OWN YouTube Channel.

[12] Ewalt, DM. (2007, Oct 9). "When I Grow Up: Kids' Dream Job Salaries." www.forbes.com. https://www.forbes.com/2007/10/09/kids-dream-jobs-ent-dream1007-cx_de_1009salary.html?sh=2eaec15d74ce

Chapter 2

[13] Green, D. (2021). *Napoleon Hill My Mentor.* G&D Media. Doyle, P. (2019, Oct. 24). "Musicians on musicians," www.rollingstone.com. https://www.rollingstone.com/music/music-features/elton-john-lana-del-rey-musicians-on-musicians-cover-902354/members. thinkandgrowthrich.shop/film Napoleon Hill Think and Grow Rich Community, Facebook, November 12, 2016; extracted April 3, 2022.

[14] Canfield, J. (2015). *The Success Principles.* William Morrow, 10th edition.

[15] Green, D. (2021).

[16] Ibid.

[17] Ibid.

Chapter 3

[18] Oprah Winfrey commencement address, Stanford University, June 15, 2008.

[19] Lima, J.K. (2021). *Believe It.* Gallery Books.

[20] Ibid.

[21] Smerconish, M. (2009). *Instinct: The Man Who Stopped the 20th Hijacker.* The Lyons Press.

[22] Ibid.

Chapter 4

[23] Harvey, S. (2015). *Act like a success, think like a success.* Amistad.

[24] Ibid.

[25] Harvey, S. (2016). *Jump.* Amistad.

[26] Ibid.

[27] Steve Harvey, Wikipedia. https://en.wikipedia.org/wiki/Steve_Harvey. Accessed February 12, 2022. https://www.celebritynetworth.com/richest-celebrities/richest-comedians/steve-harvey-net-worth/. Extracted 2021, February 13.

[28] Steve Harvey commencement speech, Alabama State University, May 9, 2016.

[29] Feloni, R. (2015, June 25). "KFC Founder Colonel Sanders didn't achieve his remarkable rise to success until his 60s." Businessinsider. com. https://www.businessinsider.com/how-kfc-founder-colonel-sanders-achieved-success-in-his-60s-2015-6

[30] Thomas, D. (2015). *Dave's Way*. The Dave Thomas Foundation.

[31] Engardio, J. (June 1997). "Colonel Sanders Saved Me," *POV Magazine*. Available on Engardio YouTube Channel.

[32] Sealy, G. (2006, Jan. 7) "Obese man sues fast-food chains." abcnews. go.com, https://abcnews.go.com/US/story?id=91427&page=1

[33] "Fast Food Lawsuits." *Your World with Neil Cavuto. Fox News.* June 18, 2003.

[34] Carpenter C. & Tello-Trillo D. (2015). "Do Cheeseburger Bills Work? Effects of Tort Reform for Fast Food," *The Journal of Law and Economics,* vol 58(4), pages 805-827.

[35] www.opensecrets.org, 2004 campaign cycle.

Chapter 5

[36] Adam Siddiq interviews Jack Canfield, "A Q&A with Jack Canfield" for the *Soulfully Optimized Life Podcast,* Oct 17, 2017.

[37] "Short stories an inspiration for publisher." (1998, July 12). *Tampa Bay Times.* https://www.tampabay.com/archive/1998/07/12/short-stories-an-inspiration-for-publisher/

[38] Steinman, J. (2000, Oct 21). "Candidates hopping on issue of frog statue." *Orlando Sentinel.* https://www.orlandosentinel.com/news/os-xpm-2000-10-21-0010210530-story.html

[39] Maxwell, S. (2000, Nov 8). "Mr. Keller goes to Washington." *Orlando Sentinel.* https://www.orlandosentinel.com/news/os-xpm-2000-11-08-0011080417-story.html

[40] Cellania, M. (2012, Nov 12). "Helen Keller: Vaudeville Star." neatorama.com; originally published in *Uncle John's 24-Karat Bathroom Reader.* https://www.neatorama.com/2012/11/12/Helen-Keller-Vaudeville-Star/

Chapter 6

[41] Harvey, S. (2016). *Jump.* Amistad.

[42] Steve Harvey commencement speech, Alabama State University, 2016.

[43] Ibid.

[44] Ibid.

[45] Harvey, S. (2016). *Jump.* Amistad.

[46] Wambach, A. (2019). *Wolfpack.* Celadon.

[47] Wambach, A. (2017). *Forward.* Day Street Books.

[48] Ibid.

Chapter 7

[49] McChrystal, SA. (2014). *My share of the task.* Portfolio.

[50] McRaven WH. (2019). *Sea Stories.* Grand Central Publishing. Obama, B. (2020). *A promised land.* Crown Publishing.

Chapter 8

[51] Zaldivar, G. (2013, Feb 11). "Seal Team 6 received 'Hoosiers' pep talk before killing Osama bin Laden." Bleacherreport.com, https://bleacherreport.com/articles/1525093-seal-team-6-received-hoosiers-pep-talk-before-killing-osama-bin-laden

[52] Babcock, I. (2013, March 6). "Forgotten Experiment Resurrects the Senator." orangeobserver.com, https://www.orangeobserver.com/article/forgotten-experiment-resurrects-senator

[53] Malaea, M. (2019, Oct 8). "Florida woman who killed 5th oldest tree in the world arrested again." Newsweek. https://www.newsweek.com/florida-woman-who-killed-5th-oldest-tree-world-arrested-again-1463994

[54] https://www.seminolecountyfl.gov/core/fileparse.php/3306/urlt/an-ode-to-the-big-tree.pdf. Permission for use granted by Paul Peterzell.

[55] Lisa Kudrow commencement address, Vassar College, June 4, 2010

Chapter 9

[56] Steve Jobs commencement address, Stanford University, June 14, 2005.

[57] Baumgartner JC, Morris JS, and Coleman JM, "Did the road to the White House run through Letterman?" *Journal of Political Marketing.* (Oct 1, 2015.)

[58] Hoption C, Barling J, Turner N. "It's not you. It's me: transformational leadership and self-deprecating humor." *Leadership and Organization Development Journal* (2013).

[59] Justice Samuel Alito testified at a hearing on federal judicial compensation before the House Judiciary Committee on April 19, 2007.

[60] *"Queen teases Bush over verbal gaffe."* (2007, May 9). www.theguardion.com. https://www.theguardian.com/world/2007/may/09/usa.monarchy

[61] Ibid.

[62] Schlesinger, *A. Robert Kennedy and his times.* (Houghton Mifflin Co. 2012)

Chapter 10

[63] "New Administration: All He Asked." Time. (1961, Feb 3).

[64] Clark, D. *The Long Game: How to Be a Long-Term Thinker in a Short-Term World,* (Harvard Business Review Press 2021.)

[65] Ibid.

[66] Ibid.

[67] Ibid.

[68] Thomas, E. *First: Sandra Day O'Connor.* (Random House 2019)

[69] Ibid.

[70] "Roberts confirmed as Chief Justice." (2005, Sept 29). CBS News. https://www.cbsnews.com/news/roberts-confirmed-as-chief-justice/

[71] Persaud, B. (2006, Oct 29). "Orlando woman's plight imperils Vietnam trade efforts." *Orlando Sentinel.* https://www.orlandosentinel.com/news/os-xpm-2006-10-29-vietnam29-story.html

[72] McKay, R. (2006, Oct 29). "Keller, Stuart count on ads as race enters final days." *Orlando Sentinel.* https://www.orlandosentinel.com/news/os-xpm-2006-10-29-campaign29-story.html

[73] Liz McCausland's conversation with the author, Nov 20, 2006.

[74] Congressional Record—Senate, Dec 8, 2006, pg S11592, "The Value of Freedom" speech on Senate Floor by Senator Mel Martinez (R-FL).

Chapter 11

[75] Williams, P and Babcock, M. *Tom Osbourne on Leadership: Life Lessons from a Three-Time National Championship Coach.* Advantage Media Group 2012), pp 169-175.

[76] Ibid.

[77] Anderson, C. *Intelligence Isn't Enough: A Black Professional's Guide to Thriving in the Workplace.* (Jonathan Ball 2021).

[78] Ibid.

[79] Ibid.

[80] Ibid.

Chapter 12

[81] Harvey, S. *Act Like a Success, Think Like a Success* (2015)

[82] Ibid.

[83] "The 25 greatest radio and television talk show hosts of all time." (Sept 2022). *Talkers Magazine.* https://talkers.com/greatest/.

[84] Larry King commencement address, University of San Diego, July 12, 2011.

[85] Ibid.

[86] Ibid.

[87] Ibid.

[88] Netflix, Wikipedia. https://en.wikipedia.org/wiki/Netflix. Accessed January 31, 2022.

[89] Hastings, R and Meyer, E. *No Rule Rules: Neflix and the Culture of Reinvention,* (Penguin Press 2020)

[90] Ibid.

[91] Ibid.

[92] Paulson, HM Jr. *On the brink.* (Business Plus 2010).

[93] Ibid.

[94] "Top 10 Dow Jones Drops." (2008, Sept 29). Time.http://content.time.com/time/specials/packages/article/0,28804,1845523_1845619_1845541,00.html

Chapter 13

[95] Babcock, M. *Heart of a Husker: Tom Osborne's Nebraska Legacy.* (Sports Publishing 2006).

[96] Ibid.

[97] Ibid.

[98] Williams, P and Babcock, M. (2012) *Tom Osborne on Leadership.*

[99] Keller, R. (2020, Nov 20). "What I learned at the Harvard IOP's Congressional Orientation," The Harvard Crimson, https://www.thecrimson.com/article/2020/11/30/keller-iop-congressional-orientation/

Chapter 14

[100] "The Families Bush and Kennedy." (2001, Nov 30). *New York Times.*

[101] Starr, K. *The Starr Report: Official Report of the Independent Counsel's Investigation of the President.* (Prima Pub 1998), p. 183, "From 9:53 to 10:14 p.m., he [Clinton] spoke with Rep H.L. "Sonny" Callahan."

[102] Hays, CL. (2004, July 17). "Martha Stewart's Sentence." New York Times. https://www.nytimes.com/2004/07/17/business/martha-stewart-s-sentence-overview-5-months-jail-stewart-vows-ll-be-back.html

[103] Baker, P. (2018, April 18). "In Barbara Bush's final days, faith, courage, and a little last needling." New York Times. https://www.nytimes.com/2018/04/18/us/politics/george-w-bush-interview-barbara-bush-death-.html

[104] "Split rulings on the ten commandments displays." (2005, June 27). nbcnews.com. https://www.nbcnews.com/id/wbna8375948

Epilogue

[105] Brinnel, D. "Bad Advice Bears," on "Dave's Creative" YouTube Channel. Kudos to Mr. Brinnel for his very funny, tongue-in-cheek segment on bear safety tips. His website is www.davebrinnel.com.

[106] Alvarez, T. "9 Bear Safety Tips from a Bear Biologist." (2017, Sept 28). backpacker.com, https://www.backpacker.com/survival/the-truth-about-bears-the-skills/

[107] Nicolle, E. (2019). *Bears Want to Kill You: The Authoritative Guide to Survival in the War Between Man and Bear.* Mr. Nicolle is a talented comic book creator, artist, and writer with a very unique and highly specialized niche in the field of bear safety humor. His website is www.bearmageddon.com.

About the Author

Former U.S. Congressman Ric Keller served eight years in the U.S. House of Representatives. He chaired the House Higher Education subcommittee and served on the Judiciary and Education committees.

Today he is an attorney, writer, humorist, and television commentator. His TEDx Talk, "The Power of Self-Deprecating Humor," was the sixth most-watched TEDx Talk in the world in May 2022. Ric received his bachelor's degree from East Tennessee State University, where he graduated first in his class, and his law degree from Vanderbilt Law School.

In his free time, Ric loves riding motorcycles, reading, and going to concerts, comedy clubs, and football games. He lives in Winter Park, Florida with his wife, Lori, and their blended family. His website is www.rickeller.net.